TRANSFORM STRESS, CRISIS, & TRAUMA THROUGH CREATIVITY

AN ART THERAPY & WRITING WORKBOOK TO ACTIVATE WELLBEING STRATEGIES

Anita B. Rankin, MA, ATR, CPT
Mary Michola Fibich, MA, ATR

This publication is designed to provide accurate information regarding the subject matter covered. It is sold with the understanding that the authors are not engaged in providing psychological or other professional services through this medium. If such professional advice or service is required, the services of a competent professional should be sought. The purpose of this workbook is to educate, inform, and enlighten those persons who wish to use the art and creative writing processes for self-understanding, or those who may be working with such individuals professionally. Legal disclaimer: The authors will have neither liability nor responsibility to any person or entity with respect to any loss or damage caused, or alleged to be caused, directly or indirectly, by the information in this book. Readers of this publication agree that neither author will be held responsible or liable for damages that may be alleged as resulting directly or indirectly from the use of this publication.

Copyright © 2024 by Anita B. Rankin, Mary Michola Fibich
All rights reserved.

For information, contact Sidran Press, Traumatic Stress Institute of Klingberg Family Centers, 370 Linwood Street, New Britain, CT 06052.

Printed and distributed by Off the Common Books, Amherst, MA

ISBN: 978-1-951928-88-9

This workbook is dedicated to all the clients we have worked with who bravely sought support as they faced stress, crises, and trauma. Each person put trust in us and was open to investing in the art and creative writing interventions we offered. This workbook incorporates the feedback, insights, and wisdom they shared with us.

CONTENTS

preface	7
introduction	8
how to use this book	11

project 1
ONE-OF-A-KIND COLLAGE   stress & strengths — 13

project 2
GIVE SHAPE TO EVERYDAY STRESS   strife & strategies — 19

project 3
SPIRALS OF HUMANITY   commonality & compassion — 29

project 4
ALONG THESE LINES OF THOUGHT   mindfulness & acceptance — 37

project 5
CAST AN EVER-WIDER NET   interconnections & reflections — 43

project 6
READ MOTION INTO EMOTION   description & imagination — 55

project 7
SENSORY AWARENESS DIPTYCH   relaxation & regeneration — 63

project 8
WABI-SABI SENSE-OF-SELF   imperfection & authenticity — 71

project 9
RISE ABOVE A RED TIDE OF UNCERTAINTY   choice & action — 83

project 10
SURREALISM FOR THE SAKE OF GOODNESS   curiosity & exploration — 89

project 11
DEPICT AND RESCRIPT YOUR INNER CRITIC   liberation & transformation — 97

project 12
UNFOLD A CRISIS-PROPELLED PLAN   options & outcomes — 115

project **13**
ENLIVEN THE TEXTURE OF YOUR LIFE   enhancement & change   125

project **14**
IN AND OUT OF A MAZE   trauma & aftereffects   133

project **15**
PEEL BACK THE LAYERS   anger & vulnerability   149

project **16**
PUNCH HOLES IN YOUR PAINFUL PAST   shame & guilt   157

project **17**
WALK THROUGH A WALL OF FEAR   courage & determination   167

project **18**
UPDATE AN INTERPERSONAL LANDSCAPE   respect & validation   183

project **19**
A WEAVING TO HELP WITHSTAND LOSS   consolation & endurance   191

project **20**
BALANCE ROCKS TO LIVE YOUR VALUES   purpose & meaning   199

project **21**
DECLARATIVE ART FOR COLLECTIVE TRAUMA   impact & empowerment   213

project **22**
COUNTERIMAGE YOUR WORLDVIEW   suffering & wonderment   221

project **23**
VISIONS TO FORGIVE, RECONCILE, AND HEAL   release & recovery   237

project **24**
COLOR YOUR POST-TRAUMATIC GROWTH   adaptability & resiliency   251

appendix A: WELLBEING PRACTICES   260
appendix B: NOTES FOR THERAPISTS, COUNSELORS, AND GROUP FACILITATORS   266
acknowledgements   268
about the authors   269

PREFACE

We first worked together in the 1990s as art therapists in Washington, D.C. at an inpatient and outpatient facility with adults who had experienced severe trauma. During that time, we developed inventive art therapy techniques while creating the workbook, *Managing Traumatic Stress through Art*, with Barry M. Cohen. The first edition of that workbook was published in 1995 and translated into Korean in 2003. It remains in print and continues to be a viable contribution to the field of art therapy.

Since then, we've worked separately in different locations with hundreds of individuals and groups in private practice, trauma and rape crisis centers, addiction treatment programs, medical facilities, wellness retreat centers, as well as hospice, school, corporate, and prison settings. Our creative endeavors as artists and poets have also been influential to our work as expressive arts therapists.

In 2015, recognizing the ever-increasing effects of stress in our globally connected world, we agreed it was time to collaborate on an all-new, up-to-date art therapy workbook that would combine artmaking and creative writing with current evidence-based treatment strategies.

The projects we designed for this new workbook draw inspiration from many therapeutic and treatment modalities. In addition to cognitive behavioral (CBT) and dialectical-behavior (DBT) treatment methods, we have applied selected theories and practices from positive psychology, compassion-focused therapy (CFT), acceptance and commitment therapy (ACT), and somatic therapies, along with recent research in neuroscience, mindfulness, and creativity.

We developed and revised this workbook over a period of seven years while working with individuals and groups in treatment for trauma, addiction, depression, anxiety, and other physical and mental health conditions. A variety of people, including students, educators, business leaders, factory workers, healthcare staff, law enforcement personnel, military veterans, therapists, artists, writers, and retirees reported achieving therapeutic gains as a result of completing projects from this workbook.

Collaborating from opposite sides of the country, we bring our combined knowledge and experience to you in this creative workbook. We believe these innovative art and writing projects will provide you with tools to manage and transform the effects of everyday stress, crises, and traumatic experiences while inspiring you to expand your creative ability, not only to improve your own wellbeing but also to envision a better future for our world.

Anita B. Rankin, MA, ATR, CPT
Mary Michola Fibich, MA, ATR

INTRODUCTION

This workbook offers guidelines to transform everyday stress, crises, and the aftereffects of trauma through artmaking and creative writing. It's designed for adults and teenagers to use at home on their own, with therapists, or in group settings. Previous art or creative writing experience isn't necessary to successfully complete these projects. Individuals who have a background in art or creative writing can bring their own distinct style to the creative processes and products.

Art therapists, counselors, psychotherapists, social workers, and life coaches can also use this workbook as a valuable resource in their work with individuals and groups. To supplement learning and training, mental health and expressive arts therapy students will find this workbook helpful as well.

Each project begins with an information page relevant to the topic. Examples of completed artworks are included to stimulate curiosity, imagination, and creativity and to ease doubts for beginning artmakers. A list of materials and preparations are followed by step-by-step instructions for artmaking and writing. Images are provided in the workbook to be used in some of the projects to facilitate artmaking. Questions help readers to gain understanding of the topic as it applies to their own circumstances. The Life Applications section provides suggestions and questions for readers to individualize and solidify choices for positive change.

Stress, Crisis, & Trauma

Stress is an unavoidable part of being human and alive in today's world. It's an emotional, mental, and physical response to demanding and difficult events and situations. We regularly experience or witness personal, family, community, and global adversity that can affect us over short or longer periods of time. Stress is often seen as a negative factor in our lives, but it can also be understood as a form of creative energy that can propel us forward in positive ways.

A crisis is a higher-stress event or situation, typically lasting at least four to six weeks. It pushes and presses us into a state of disequilibrium and disorganization, marking a critical turning point. Disruption in normal patterns of functioning and difficulty in coping are common. Most people need the support of outside resources to deal with a crisis.

Trauma is the most severe form of stress. It overwhelms normal coping mechanisms and ruptures beliefs about self, others, and the world. Trauma may occur as a one-time event or an ongoing situation in which actual or threatened injury or death occurs. It's often associated with interpersonal violations such as assault, rape, domestic and sexual violence, and severe childhood neglect and abuse; with direct experience of natural or man-made disasters including fires, hurricanes, earthquakes, vehicular or toxic waste accidents; with life-threatening medical conditions; and with war or terrorist-related exposure. Following trauma, many survivors won't be able to resume life as it was before, but for those who are able to accept the resulting changes and create revised ways of being in the world, increased resiliency and personal growth may result.

With individual trauma, a single person is the primary focus of the trauma, even though others close to that person may be affected. Collective trauma differs from individual trauma in that it's an event or situation shared by a specific group of people. Collective trauma may occur in small groups, communities, cultures, countries, regions, and throughout the world. Causes of collective trauma include—but are not limited to—war exposure, mass shootings, genocide, natural and man-made disasters, epidemics, widespread famine, and violence associated with oppression, racism, religious discrimination, and other human rights violations.

There are no clearly drawn lines between everyday stress, crisis, and trauma. Each stressful event or situation is unique, as is each person who experiences that event or situation. Environmental, cultural, genetic, and age factors, as well as previous and current life experiences, will influence whether an individual will categorize any given situation as stress, crisis, or trauma.

Awareness, Acceptance, & Exploration

When we're stressed, we tend to constrict both physically and mentally. Our muscles tighten and our brains overload with excess input. Even if we continue to function, we may not be able to live in ways we'd prefer. Negative and repetitive patterns of perceiving and reacting may keep us from reaching goals and honoring our values.

To interrupt and break free from these impairing patterns, we start by increasing our awareness of what is happening in our lives now. Without judgment, we accept the present moment as it is and accept ourselves as we are. We explore what has happened in the past to gain greater understanding of causes and conditions that are contributing to our current stress.

While acknowledging there is a certain degree of pain and difficulty that comes with being human and living in our world, we can also search for positive factors within our less than perfect circumstances and selves. We can take care of our current lives and take care of what we value now as we begin to see how we would like to live in the present and near future.

Curiosity, Imagination, & Creativity

When we're overstressed, in crisis, or caught in the aftermath of trauma, it may be hard to imagine how our lives can change. Even so, by opening our minds through curiosity, we can look a little deeper, gather more information, and gain understanding related to our stress. We can begin to imagine new options for developing strengths, wellbeing strategies, and available supports. As we increase our resilience and find ways to lessen the burden of stress, we gain access to the mental and emotional space needed to welcome increased tranquility and positive experiences into our lives.

Curiosity and imagination are precursors to creativity. Instead of a simplistic left/right brain explanation of creativity, current neuroscience research indicates that multiple regions and complex circuitries in our brains are at play. Our incredibly complicated brains contain over 100 billion neurons and 100 trillion synaptic connections to allow a higher level of creativity as compared to other species on our planet. No matter what has happened to us, creativity is a vital tool to re-envision and reinvent our lives and ourselves beyond what we previously thought possible.

Artmaking, Writing, & Transformation

One way to open our curiosity, imagination, and creativity is through artmaking. Art has been intrinsic to human expression since prehistoric times. It gives line, shape, and color to thoughts and emotions that don't have physical form in themselves. Artmaking lends a sense of control to what often seems out of control and allows us to view others, the world, and ourselves in relatively non-threatening and innovative ways. Many people find it hard to voice painful thoughts and feelings related to their stress. Artmaking provides an alternative form of expression.

Creative writing helps us to clarify and organize our thoughts. It enhances imagination and expands meaning, allowing us to venture farther into our creative minds. We can see into metaphoric images and read into metaphoric words to double-down on our growing awareness and transformation. In this workbook, therapeutic gains are reinforced when two creative modalities, artmaking and creative writing, interact with each other.

When creativity takes form in art and writing, we can literally see transformations as they happen within our minds and through our own hands. Once we consciously observe this, we begin to understand how art processes are like life processes. In much the same way that we create art, it's also possible to create our lives. When we live our lives in more creative ways, we aren't driven as much by the past. We're more open and flexible in the present moment and more resilient and mindful when facing future challenges.

As you work through these projects, bring playful effort to your artmaking and writing. Be curious and courageous. Without judgment, engage your creative spirit in conscious choice making. Allow yourself to indulge in the creative process as you take steps to move in the right direction toward living a more creative, less stressful life.

HOW TO USE THIS WORKBOOK

On average, it takes one to two hours to finish each project, but the length of time may vary according to each person's own pace. Projects can be done in more than one sitting for those who prefer to do so or if available time is limited.

Completing projects in their numbered sequence is preferable as creative skills and wellbeing strategies build on each other from the beginning to the end of the workbook, however projects can also be done in any order if wanted or needed. They can be repeated more than once to boost personal growth and address changing life circumstances.

The authors have provided images in the workbook for several projects. If you prefer to keep these images in the workbook, want to utilize images printed on both sides of the pages, or wish to do projects more than once, you can make photocopies of these images or trace over the simpler ones.

Art materials and the size of artworks are kept to a minimum to reduce cost, decrease potential for messy outcomes, and provide easier transportability and storage. The authors have drawn on their extensive experience with various art materials in therapy to develop these projects so artmakers are able to create and express in a manner that promotes safety, grounding, and balance.

Materials needed to complete all 24 projects are listed below:

- pencil and eraser
- ruler
- 1 black ultra-fine pen
- 1 black chisel-tip marker
- scissors
- glue stick
- 9"x12" white mixed media or drawing paper, 30 sheets
- 9"x12" tracing paper, 10 sheets
- 8½"x11" or 9"x12" assorted solid-color papers, cardstock is preferable
- oil pastels, set of 50
- paper towels
- sources for collage images such as used magazines, books, newspapers, brochures, catalogs, old calendars, greeting cards, photocopies, online printouts, and your own photos
- found or recycled papers such as used bags, maps, envelopes, notebook pads, wrapping and artist's papers, waste papers, or any paper product that will adhere with a glue stick

For higher quality artwork, we suggest using the above art materials. However, if budget constraints are an issue, you can make the following substitutions:

8½"x11" white copy paper instead of 9"x12" white mixed media or drawing paper
solid-color construction paper instead of solid-color cardstock
a set of 12 or 25 oil pastels instead of a set of 50 oil pastels

It may be helpful to keep these art materials in a box or bin for easy access.
A sink or water source is *not* necessary to complete these projects.

project 1

ONE-OF-A-KIND COLLAGE

stress & strengths

Each of our unique genetics and life experiences guarantee that we're truly one-of-a-kind human beings. Almost everything we do and create in our daily lives reflects this individuality. If a hundred people followed the directions featured in this art project using the same images and art supplies, no two artworks would be exactly alike or hold the same meaning for the artmakers.

During our lives, we develop our own personal mix of strengths that contribute to our distinct identities and the ways we function in the world. Because we routinely use our strengths without being aware of them, we're rarely conscious of how often we call on them.

Similar to using our physical strengths, the more we exercise our character strengths, the stronger and more resilient we become. We're able to intentionally develop new strengths, discover additional ways to use our strengths, and combine our strengths in different ways to formulate stress-reducing and life-enhancing strategies.

In this project, you'll identify your top five personal strengths and create a collage to represent two small goals: one using strengths to reduce stress and one using them to enhance a positive activity in your life. You'll add folded squares of white paper to your artwork that resemble wings, kites, or sails to symbolize your strengths rising to the occasion and helping you to navigate through the world. As a short creative writing exercise, you'll give your artwork an intriguing title.

PREPARATIONS

- Clear and protect the surface of your artmaking table.
- Gather tools and materials: pen or pencil for writing
  ruler
  scissors
  glue stick
  9"x12" white mixed media paper, 2 sheets
  image sources, such as used magazines, books, newspapers, brochures, catalogs, old calendars, greeting cards, photocopies, online printouts, or your own photos

- Minimize noise and the potential for interruptions.
- You may opt to work on this project in more than one sitting.
- If you experience a notable increase in your stress level while doing this project, take a break.
- As you follow directions, be curious and open to what occurs. Refrain from judging the correctness or quality of your artwork and writing.
- If it's comfortable to do so, close your eyes and consciously enjoy three breaths, being aware of the air moving through your nose or the subtle expansion and contraction of your diaphragm.
- Notice where your body is contacting the chair, floor, or table. Look around the room. Experience a sense of being present in your body and surroundings as you begin.

DIRECTIONS

step 1
Identify one of the following strengths you've used today. _____

courage	imagination	open-mindedness	hope	honesty	friendliness	practicality	determination
wisdom	resilience	self-acceptance	faith	integrity	enthusiasm	efficiency	willpower
intuition	endurance	self-regulation	grace	fairness	playfulness	competency	forgiveness
curiosity	adaptability	receiving support	humor	kindness	intelligence	productivity	gratitude
learning	willingness	giving support	energy	devotion	optimism	teamwork	mindfulness
creativity	flexibility	problem-solving	love	patience	spirituality	leadership	humility

Describe how you specifically used this strength.

_____

_____

step 2
Almost everyone has at least a small measure of each strength listed in step 1, including you. But your most frequently used strengths are the ones that contribute the most to your unique identity and ways of being in the world. Circle five strengths listed in step 1 that you consider to be your top strengths, the strengths you use the most, or the ones that are most important to you.

step 3

Cut seven 2"x 2" squares from a sheet of white mixed media paper.

Fold the squares diagonally in half so they become triangular shapes. Inside each of five of these folded squares, write one of the strengths you circled from the list in step 1.

Imagine these folded squares are wings, kites, or sails. Think of them as your strengths rising to the occasion or helping you to navigate through the world to transform stress and enhance positive activities in your life.

step 4

Note one situation in your current life that is causing you to experience mild to moderate stress.

_____

_____

Look through image sources (listed in the *PREPARATIONS* section) for an abstract, semi-abstract, or realistic image to represent this stressor or how this stress makes you feel. This image may contain colors, shapes, lines, people, animals, indoor or outdoor scenes, natural or man-made objects, art reproductions, or other types of visual elements.

Why did you choose this image?

_____

_____

From the strengths you circled in step 1, which of those strengths might be helpful in reducing the stress you noted above?

_____

Is there a strength you didn't circle that could be helpful to reduce this specific stress?

If so, which strength is it? _____ Write the name of this strength inside another one of the blank folded squares.

step 5

Identify a current activity in your life that has a positive effect on you, such as a hobby, walking, looking at the sky, cooking, reading, playing with children or pets, watching a funny show, talking to a good friend, volunteering, etc.

_____

Look through image sources (listed in the *PREPARATIONS* section) for an abstract, semi-abstract, or realistic image to represent this positive activity or how this activity makes you feel. This image may contain colors, shapes, lines, people, animals, indoor or outdoor scenes, natural or man-made objects, art reproductions, or other types of visual elements.

Why did you choose this image?

_____

_____

From the list in step 1, identify strengths you use that contribute to this positive activity.

_____

Write them inside the last blank folded square.

step 6

Begin to arrange the two images you selected, along with all or some of the folded squares on a sheet of white paper in a way that is meaningful to you. Trim or cut the collage elements however you wish. You may want to overlap the images, place them side-by-side, or keep them separate. The folded squares can be placed on top of the images, to the side, or anywhere else that seems right.

When you're satisfied with the arrangement, glue all the elements to the sheet of white paper, allowing the folded squares to stay partially open so you can read the words written inside.

What is the significance of the way you arranged the images and folded squares?

_____

_____

_____

_____

step 7

In this step you'll be writing an intriguing title for your artwork. Following are three titles of the artwork examples at the beginning of this project:

>*Super-Impositions Collide Outside the Circle of Mindfulness*

>*Adaptability Flies on Air, Imagination Wings on Ideas, Willpower Sails on Water*

>*Heritage Discarded, Untie Trash, Turn to Compost, Feed Flowers, Have Hope*

Look at your artwork from a distance, then up close to see the details. Read your written strength words out loud. To title your artwork you might want to use one or more of your strength words combined with a description of the images. Play around with the words until you're satisfied that your title is intriguing and/or meaningful. Write your title on the line below.

_____

LIFE APPLICATIONS

- To transform the stress you described in step 4, identify one of your strengths that will be helpful. Exactly how, when, and where will you apply this strength to reduce your stress?

  _____
  _____
  _____
  _____

- To enhance or add a positive activity to your life, specify one of your strengths that will be useful. Exactly how, when, and where will you apply this strength?

  _____
  _____
  _____
  _____

- Feel free to do this project as often as you like.

CONCLUSIONS

- Note any useful insights, revelations, beliefs, or intentions that emerged while you worked on this project or that come to mind now.

  _____
  _____
  _____

- Detect any tension you're holding in your neck, shoulders, or elsewhere in your body. Consciously relax, pat, massage, or gently stretch those areas.
- If it's comfortable to do so, close your eyes and consciously enjoy three breaths.
- Notice where your body is contacting the chair, floor, or table. Look around the room. Experience a sense of being present in your body and surroundings as you finish.
- Sign and date your artwork. Store it for safekeeping.

project 2

GIVE SHAPE TO EVERYDAY STRESS
strife & strategies

Stress is a normal part of our everyday lives. It's unrealistic to believe we can live stress-free. If we try to avoid or deny stress, we may experience a degree of short-term relief, but in the long run unaddressed stress often accumulates to make things worse. This may result in maladaptive or addictive behaviors, such as excessive shopping, television-watching, video-gaming, or constant online activity. Adverse eating habits as well as alcohol or drug misuse may also occur.

Instead of believing that all stress drains our life force, we can view stress as a form of raw energy that keeps us moving in the right direction. There are times when our stress is related to improving our lives and the lives of others. Examples of positive stressors are attempting to master new skills, pursuing hard-to-obtain goals, or engaging with someone or something that gives meaning to our lives despite the difficulties.

There are five basic tactics to manage everyday stress:

- Improve physical self-care through exercise, good nutrition, and adequate sleep.
- Revise daily tasks, schedules, and supports.
- Practice conscious breathing and muscle relaxation.
- Add pleasant sensory experiences and enjoyable activities to each day.
- Re-envision stress as creative energy for achieving goals.

Even if difficult life circumstances cannot be improved immediately, we can find small ways to soothe and lower the level of our stress.

In this project, you'll cut and arrange simple geometric shapes to represent your everyday stress, then add more shapes to symbolize three basic tactics to manage your stress. Using words you've written and circled in response to questions, you'll complete a fill-in-the-blanks poem on strife and striving in your life.

PREPARATIONS

- Clear and protect the surface of your artmaking table.
- Gather tools and materials: pencil and eraser
    scissors
    glue stick
    9"x12" white mixed media paper, 1 sheet
    8½"x11" or 9"x12" assorted solid-color papers

- Minimize noise and the potential for interruptions.
- You may opt to work on this project in more than one sitting.
- If you experience a notable increase in your stress level while doing this project, take a break.
- As you follow directions, be curious and open to what occurs. Refrain from judging the correctness or quality of your artwork and writing.
- If it's comfortable to do so, close your eyes and consciously enjoy three breaths, being aware of the air moving through your nose or the expansion and contraction of your diaphragm.
- Notice where your body is contacting the chair, floor, or table. Look around the room. Experience a sense of being present in your body and surroundings as you begin.

DIRECTIONS

step 1
Describe one way you have taken care of your physical body that occurred today or yesterday. This might be related to nutritious eating, healthy exercise, adequate sleep, or relaxation time.

_____

_____

_____

step 2
List 1-5 of your typical everyday stressors.

_____

_____

_____

_____

_____

step 3
Circle 3-5 of the following words or phrases related to your everyday stress.

pressure	tension	inner conflict	external conflict	urgency	worry
panic	overwork	distractions	procrastination	doubt	impatience
agitation	restlessness	discomfort	uneasiness	dread	irritation
boredom	chaos	responsibility	interruptions	hassles	threat
fear	loneliness	invisibility	disagreements	criticism	anger
deadline	frustration	time crunch	daily grind	self-doubt	uncertainty

Where do you feel everyday stress in your body? _____

step 4
Pick a solid-color sheet of paper to represent the level of your everyday stress.

What color did you choose? _____ Is it bright, neon, intense, dull, light, heavy, dark?

From a half-sheet of this solid-color paper, cut squares, triangles, and circles in small, medium, and larger sizes. Don't try to cut perfect shapes; irregularities and imperfections can enhance the originality of artwork. Save the scraps.

step 5
To experiment with different ways of arranging shapes and scraps, first place them toward the edges of a sheet of white mixed media paper. Notice the empty white space in the center of the white paper.

Next, shove the shapes and scraps to the center of the white paper. They will overlap and jut up against each other. Notice the open white space around the edges of the white paper.

Finally, hold the shapes and scraps about a foot above the white paper. Let them drop. Some of the shapes may scatter off the white paper. Notice the random quality of this arrangement along with the varied white spaces.

Remove all the shapes and scraps from the white paper. Using some or all of them, place them on the white paper, arranging and rearranging them until you're satisfied the composition represents your everyday stress. Glue the shapes to the white paper.

Is there a reason you arranged the shapes in the way you did? _____

step 6

Look at the shapes in your artwork. Circle 3-5 of the following words that metaphorically describe them.

ROUNDED / CURVED SHAPES: dot   drop   molecule   splotch   blotch   egg
spot   button   cloud   coin   token   wafer   blister   marble   lump
bump   disk   dollop   glob   blob   wad   hole   balloon   ball
bubble   puddle   pond   pool   lake   pebble   stone   rock   boulder
arena   sphere   globe   planet   moon   sun   orb   cake   wave

SQUARE / RECTANGULAR SHAPES: nugget   block   patch   cube   slab   section
brick   box   loaf   table   bar   hunk   chunk   plank   pocket   stick
pouch   book   pedestal   bag   beam   ledge   shelf   door   window

TRIANGULAR / ANGULAR SHAPES: pointer   cursor   spike   slice   sliver   bite
portion   wedge   chip   spur   prong   lance   arrow   thorn   tent   peak
mountain   harpoon   ramp   projectile   pivot   tooth   cone   tree   funnel   party
indicator   pyramid   hat   campfire   fulcrum   pinnacle

SCRAPS / ODD SHAPES: shred   snippet   splinter   ring   bracelet   arch   bits
pieces   notch   arc   crescent   frame   clutter   shard   loop   handcuff   knot
fragment   arena   star   debris   rubble   dreck   junk   cage   necklace   hook

22

step 7

Practice the following steps for self-compassion.

1. I acknowledge how difficult my everyday stress can be.
2. I offer myself a kind thought or soothing gesture.

EXAMPLES OF SELF-COMPASSIONATE THOUGHTS:

This stress is hard for me right now.
It's ok to give attention to myself.
I can get through this safely.
My strengths and values can help me.
I give gentle warmth and caring to myself.
I can show up for myself no matter what.
I respect myself.
I can be a supportive friend to myself.
I offer myself reassurance.
I offer encouragement to myself.

This may not be as bad as I think.
I can let go of unnecessary suffering.
This is how it is for now; it might get better.
I remind myself that everything is impermanent.
There may be positive aspects to this stress.
It's understandable why this affects me.
I can give myself a break.
I give myself permission to relax.
I offer concern and comfort to myself.
I allow myself to feel hope.

Considering the everyday stress you described in step 2, offer a kind thought to yourself by writing it on the blank line below. It may be one or a combination of the above thoughts or a thought you create for yourself now.

_____

EXAMPLES OF SELF-COMPASSIONATE GESTURES:

Massage my face and jaw.
Pat my head.
Soothe my forehead.
Take a short walk outside or inside.
Drink a glass of water or cup of tea.
Take a soothing bath or shower.
Exercise.
Make a bowl of soup.
Eat a healthy snack.
Feel the outside air or breeze on my face.
Take a rest or a nap.
Give myself flowers.

Hold my hand over my heart.
Gently massage my stomach.
Hug myself.
Hold my own hand.
Take a conscious breath.
Read an inspirational passage.
Tap my shoulders with my fingertips.
Listen to comforting music.
Look up at the sky.
Watch the sunrise or sunset.
Go to a quiet place.
Cross my arms over my chest.

What is one of the above gestures or a different soothing gesture you can initiate now, when you take a break, or when you finish this project?

_____

3. I know other people in the world are experiencing similar stress; I'm not alone.
4. In my mind, I send compassionate thoughts to all those people, far and near.

step 8

Your breath is a built-in tool to manage stress. It's always available to you no matter where you are. Pausing to take one or more conscious breaths can help relieve your stress.

You can simply pay attention to one or two normal cycles of inhalation and exhalation. Or you can practice the following technique, which may have the added effect of slightly lowering your heart rate and blood pressure.

Breathe in normally through your nose. Breathe out through pursed lips. Repeat 1-3 times.

step 9

Select a solid-color paper to represent conscious breathing. What color did you choose? _____

Cut this color into a small geometric or free-form shape. Why did you cut it into this specific shape?

_____

_____

Refer to the word lists in step 6. What metaphoric word describes this "breathing" shape? _____

Set this shape aside for now.

step 10

Consciously take a moment to relax your muscles through gentle movements, massage, stretching, or walking.

Choose a solid-color paper to represent this loosening and relaxing. What color did you choose? _____

Cut a small geometric or free-form shape from this color. Why did you cut it into this specific shape?

_____

Refer to the word lists in step 6. What metaphoric word describes this shape? _____

Set this shape aside for now.

step 11

All of us experience inadequacies or lapses in our physical self-care. It takes time and effort to maintain our physical bodies, but if you make the effort, you'll lower your everyday stress in the long run.

What is one small realistic change you can make to improve your physical self-care? Consider your diet and hydration, exercise, sleep routine, or medical and dental check-ups and follow-ups.

_____

Exactly when and how will you activate this improvement?

_____
_____
_____
_____

Select a solid-color paper to represent this physical self-care improvement. Cut this color into a small shape.

Refer to the word lists in step 6. What metaphoric word describes this shape? _____

step 12

Gather the three small shapes you have cut in steps 9, 10, and 11. Move them around on your artwork until you're satisfied with the arrangement. Glue them to the surface.

step 13

Look at your artwork. Turn it sideways and upside down to see which way you like it best.

Now focus on the white space instead of the solid-color shapes. Let your eyes move through the white space. For a moment, allow your eyes to rest in one area within the white space. Consider what that white space might mean to you. Circle any of the following words that apply.

clarity	openness	grace	sanctuary	stillness	tranquility
patience	airiness	faith	refuge	open-mindedness	mindfulness
safety	renewal	silence	peace	creative possibility	vibrant spirit
clearing	resilience	quietness	purity	spaciousness	consciousness
hope	serenity	potentiality	awareness	timelessness	free energy

step 14

In this step you'll be composing a fill-in-the-blanks poem that relates to your artwork. Following are two examples of poems written by artmakers who previously completed this project.

AN ARTFUL RECKONING

Shaped by past and present, splotches, sticks, and an orange thorn squared and triangulated in my mind, circulating up and down, in and out of my body. Even so, I allow an arc of breath, pool of ease, and dollop of care to temper the burden. For this moment, I dwell in the clarity, timelessness, and refuge within and all around.

PIVOTAL MOMENT

Hot pink colors this hour, shaped by past and present: a giant beach ball balanced on the point of a pyramid, an empty arena filled with energy squared, triangulated, encircled in my body. And here, a pivot, an added shade of purple to lessen the urgency, ease the restlessness, my eyes taking measure to see through to the possibilities.

Use the provided prompts beneath the blank lines to begin composing your poem. You may want to change the form of words, add or delete phrases, or revise your poem in whatever way you wish. You can also title your poem and write or type it on a separate sheet of paper.

_____
(title)

Shaped by past and present, _____, _____,
 (Fill in these blanks and the blank below with words you circled in step 6.)

and _____,

squared and triangulated in my mind, circulating up and down, in and out of my body.

Even so, I allow a _____ *of breath,*
 (Fill in this blank with the metaphoric word written at the end of step 9.)

a _____ *of ease,*
 (Fill in this blank with the metaphoric word written at the end of step 10.)

and a _____ *of care*
 (Fill in this blank with the metaphoric word written at the end of in step 11.)

to temper the _____.
 (Fill in this blank with one or more words you circled in step 3.)

For this moment, I can dwell in the _____, _____, *and* _____
 (Fill in these blanks with circled words from step 13.)

within and all around.

Read your poem out loud so you can both see and hear it.

LIFE APPLICATIONS

- Review the five basic tactics to manage stress on page 19. What is a small improvement you can make to lower your stress that relates to one of the five tactics?

- Exactly when and how will you implement this small improvement?

- Is there something you can eliminate in your life that would lower your stress without compromising your values or goals?

- What is one small positive thing you can add to your day that could lower your stress level? Alternatively, how can you add a bit more white space to your life?

- Look back at the stressors you described in step 2. Circle any stressors that are serving to motivate you or keep you moving toward living your values or achieving your goals. Re-envision those stressors as a form of positive energy you can use to fuel your present life.

- Practice stress reduction throughout the day.
    1. Pause when you become aware you're experiencing stress.
    2. Consciously breathe and relax your muscles as much as possible.
    3. Give yourself a moment of compassion.
    4. Ask yourself if the stress you're experiencing is serving to move you forward. If it is, honor that stress as positive energy.

- You can revisit your art and writing from this project if their messages and insights can be of benefit to you. Repeat this project whenever you wish.

CONCLUSIONS

- Note any useful insights, revelations, beliefs, or intentions that emerged while you worked on this project or that come to mind now.

- Detect any tension you're holding in your neck, shoulders, or elsewhere in your body. Consciously relax, pat, massage, or gently stretch those areas.
- If it's comfortable to do so, close your eyes and consciously enjoy three breaths.
- Notice where your body is contacting the chair, floor, or table. Look around the room. Experience a sense of being present in your body and surroundings as you finish.
- Sign and date your artwork. Store it for safekeeping.

project **3**

SPIRALS OF HUMANITY

commonality & compassion

In one way or another, almost all art and creative writing speaks to being human. Through seeing or making art and reading or writing words, we increase our understanding of what it's like to be human while developing our ability to relate to ourselves, others, and the world in new and different ways.

Regardless of the many cultural and environmental differences in the world, all humans experience stress. When primary needs aren't met, for instance if food or clean water is scarce, shelter or healthcare is unavailable, or sanitation and protection from violence is inadequate, people will suffer profound stress. Lack of secondary needs, such as supportive connections with others, educational opportunities, and the ability to work to support self or family can cause serious stress.

Even when epidemics, earthquakes, hurricanes, wars, mass shootings, bombings, and refugee problems aren't directly at our doorstep, just knowing about them may contribute to our own stress levels as well as the collective stress in the world.

To alleviate some of our stress, we can practice compassion, beginning with ourselves and then extending it to family, friends, community, and the world. Compassion is not pity. Compassion is about giving kindness with the intention to help, whereas pity is about seeing humans as helpless victims. Compassion is turning to face difficulties instead of turning our backs.

Through art and writing, you'll explore personal, local, and global stressors from your own viewpoint as well as those from another person you imagine. You'll draw intersecting spirals to represent stress as a common aspect of humanity. From your observations and discoveries in this exploration, you'll get a glimpse of how our individual lives overlap and merge with the larger human story.

Included in this project are directions for a cut-and-paste creative writing experience focused on relieving stress through acknowledging common humanity, offering compassion, and extending comfort through imagination.

PREPARATIONS

- Clear and protect the surface of your artmaking table.
- Gather tools and materials: pen or pencil for writing
  9"x12" white mixed media paper, 1 sheet
  oil pastels
  paper towel
  black ultra-fine pen

- Minimize noise and the potential for interruptions.
- You may opt to work on this project in more than one sitting.
- If you experience a notable increase in your stress level while doing this project, take a break.
- As you follow directions, be curious and open to what occurs. Refrain from judging the correctness or quality of your artwork and writing.
- If it's comfortable to do so, close your eyes and consciously enjoy three breaths, being aware of the air moving through your nose or the expansion and contraction of your diaphragm.
- Notice where your body is contacting the chair, floor, or table. Look around the room. Experience a sense of being present in your body and surroundings as you begin.

DIRECTIONS

step 1
In the open air in front of you, draw invisible spirals with your fingers and hands, rotating from your wrists. Then draw bigger spirals with your arms rotating from your elbows and shoulders.

step 2
Horizontally orient a sheet of white mixed media paper. Select any dark-color oil pastel except black.

View the artwork examples at the beginning of this project for a visual reference as you follow the artmaking steps.

Starting just above the middle and slightly to the left side of the paper, draw a continuous spiral line beginning from the center of the spiral. Continue drawing the spiral line until it reaches the paper's edge.

With a black ultra-fine pen, draw a small simple star or house symbol in the center of this spiral to indicate the location where you live.

With a small piece of clean paper towel, rub over the spiral line with pressure to smooth it.

step 3
Describe one stressful situation at home or in your workplace.

_____

_____

project **3**

SPIRALS OF HUMANITY

commonality & compassion

In one way or another, almost all art and creative writing speaks to being human. Through seeing or making art and reading or writing words, we increase our understanding of what it's like to be human while developing our ability to relate to ourselves, others, and the world in new and different ways.

Regardless of the many cultural and environmental differences in the world, all humans experience stress. When primary needs aren't met, for instance if food or clean water is scarce, shelter or healthcare is unavailable, or sanitation and protection from violence is inadequate, people will suffer profound stress. Lack of secondary needs, such as supportive connections with others, educational opportunities, and the ability to work to support self or family can cause serious stress.

Even when epidemics, earthquakes, hurricanes, wars, mass shootings, bombings, and refugee problems aren't directly at our doorstep, just knowing about them may contribute to our own stress levels as well as the collective stress in the world.

To alleviate some of our stress, we can practice compassion, beginning with ourselves and then extending it to family, friends, community, and the world. Compassion is not pity. Compassion is about giving kindness with the intention to help, whereas pity is about seeing humans as helpless victims. Compassion is turning to face difficulties instead of turning our backs.

Through art and writing, you'll explore personal, local, and global stressors from your own viewpoint as well as those from another person you imagine. You'll draw intersecting spirals to represent stress as a common aspect of humanity. From your observations and discoveries in this exploration, you'll get a glimpse of how our individual lives overlap and merge with the larger human story.

Included in this project are directions for a cut-and-paste creative writing experience focused on relieving stress through acknowledging common humanity, offering compassion, and extending comfort through imagination.

PREPARATIONS

- Clear and protect the surface of your artmaking table.
- Gather tools and materials: pen or pencil for writing
  9"x12" white mixed media paper, 1 sheet
  oil pastels
  paper towel
  black ultra-fine pen

- Minimize noise and the potential for interruptions.
- You may opt to work on this project in more than one sitting.
- If you experience a notable increase in your stress level while doing this project, take a break.
- As you follow directions, be curious and open to what occurs. Refrain from judging the correctness or quality of your artwork and writing.
- If it's comfortable to do so, close your eyes and consciously enjoy three breaths, being aware of the air moving through your nose or the expansion and contraction of your diaphragm.
- Notice where your body is contacting the chair, floor, or table. Look around the room. Experience a sense of being present in your body and surroundings as you begin.

DIRECTIONS

step 1
In the open air in front of you, draw invisible spirals with your fingers and hands, rotating from your wrists. Then draw bigger spirals with your arms rotating from your elbows and shoulders.

step 2
Horizontally orient a sheet of white mixed media paper. Select any dark-color oil pastel except black.

View the artwork examples at the beginning of this project for a visual reference as you follow the artmaking steps.

Starting just above the middle and slightly to the left side of the paper, draw a continuous spiral line beginning from the center of the spiral. Continue drawing the spiral line until it reaches the paper's edge.

With a black ultra-fine pen, draw a small simple star or house symbol in the center of this spiral to indicate the location where you live.

With a small piece of clean paper towel, rub over the spiral line with pressure to smooth it.

step 3
Describe one stressful situation at home or in your workplace.

_____

_____

step 4

The areas radiating from the center of the spiral represent your neighborhood, community, town, city, state, region, or country. What is one stressful situation currently occurring in one of these areas that affects you?

_____

_____

step 5

Select one oil pastel color to represent the stressors you described in steps 3 and 4. Apply this color directly on top of the spiral line you have drawn.

With a small piece of clean paper towel, rub over the spiral line with pressure to smooth it.

step 6

Turn your artwork upside down.

With a different dark-color oil pastel, just above the middle and slightly to the left side of the paper, draw another continuous spiral line starting from the center of the spiral. Continue the spiral line until the oil pastel reaches the paper's edge. This second spiral will automatically intersect the first spiral toward the center of the paper.

With a small piece of clean paper towel, rub over the spiral line with pressure to smooth it.

step 7

Return your artwork to its original upright orientation. Using your finger as a travel guide, follow the spiral line from the center of the spiral where you live to the point where it intersects with the second spiral. From there, follow the second spiral line until you reach the center of the second spiral.

Imagine you've travelled to a part of the world you've never been to before.

When you arrive, look around. Are you in a city, suburb, town, village, in the countryside, at a shoreline, or on an island? What do you see, hear, and smell? What season is it? What is the weather and quality of air like? Are you standing or sitting? You may want to close your eyes to imagine this place in more detail. Write a description of this location on the blank lines below.

_____

_____

_____

_____

step 8

Imagine meeting a person who lives in this place. What is this person's age, gender, and race? What is this person wearing? What kind of dwelling does this person live in? Does anyone else live with this person? What are this person's main responsibilities and primary interests in life?

_____

_____

_____

_____

step 9

By speaking directly or through a translator, this person tells you about two stressors: one at home or at work and one in their community or region. What does this person tell you?

_____

_____

_____

_____

What would you like to say to this person in response?

_____

_____

_____

step 10

Select an oil pastel color to represent this person's stress described at the beginning of step 9. Apply this color directly on top of the second spiral line. Smooth this color by rubbing over it with a small clean piece of paper towel.

Do you have anything in common with this person you've imagined?

_____

_____

_____

step 11

Select an oil pastel color to represent compassion. Apply this color directly over the lines of both spirals. Smooth this color with a piece of clean paper towel.

Look at your artwork. Notice how the stress and compassion colors blend, transforming the artwork.

step 12

Again, use your finger as a travel guide, this time reversing your travels by following the spiral lines from the center of the second spiral back toward the center of the spiral where you live.

On your travels back home, imagine you discover a safe spot to rest that gives you a sense of calm and comfort. Describe what you see, hear, smell, and touch in this place.

_____

_____

_____

_____

_____

_____

_____

_____

step 13

Looking back over your writing throughout this project, circle several words and phrases you've written that draw your attention now. Write these words and phrases on a clean sheet of paper.

Cut these words and phrases out.

On another clean sheet of white paper, mix-up and reassemble these words and phrases in different ways to form new, unexpected, inventive phrases. You don't need to use all the words and phrases. When you're intrigued and satisfied with your new combinations, glue them down.

step 14

In this step you'll be creating a short piece of writing by combining the words and phrases you cut out and reassembled with any other words you wish to add.

Following are two examples of writing from artmakers who have previously completed this project.

So sorry this virus has made a home. Safety and security seem hard to find. Hope that poverty turns to wealth and opportunities visit. Heart, mind, and body fed and full. Noises and fears quiet. Colors surround and fresh air holds.

First go-round, silent risk and threat. Drawn from different colors, next round aches alone to pain even harder. Yet birds swoop; sunlight longs through pine branches. I bring tea and cookies to a clearing in this age-old forest, then meet myself through an open window.

Compose your own creative writing on the blank lines below.

LIFE APPLICATIONS

- Review the stressful situations you described in steps 3 and 4. Take a deep breath and let out a sigh. Give a kind thought to yourself. What is one small way you can provide comfort or care to yourself now?

  _____

  _____

- Practicing compassion begins with our individual selves and then extends to others.

  Below is a simple way to practice compassion for self and others.

  1. I acknowledge the stress I'm experiencing.
  2. I give myself a kind thought or gesture, such as touching my heart, soothing my forehead, or holding my own hand.
  3. I know other people in the world are experiencing similar stress; I'm not alone.
  4. In my mind, I send compassionate thoughts to those people, far and near.

- You can revisit your art and writing from this project if their messages and insights are beneficial to you. Repeat this project as often as you wish.

CONCLUSIONS

- Note any useful insights, revelations, beliefs, or intentions that emerged while you worked on this project or that come to mind now.

  _____

  _____

  _____

- Detect any tension you're holding in your neck, shoulders, or elsewhere in your body. Consciously relax, pat, massage, or gently stretch those areas.
- If it's comfortable to do so, close your eyes and consciously enjoy three breaths.
- Notice where your body is contacting the chair, floor, or table. Look around the room. Experience a sense of being present in your body and surroundings as you finish.
- Sign and date your artwork. Store it for safekeeping.

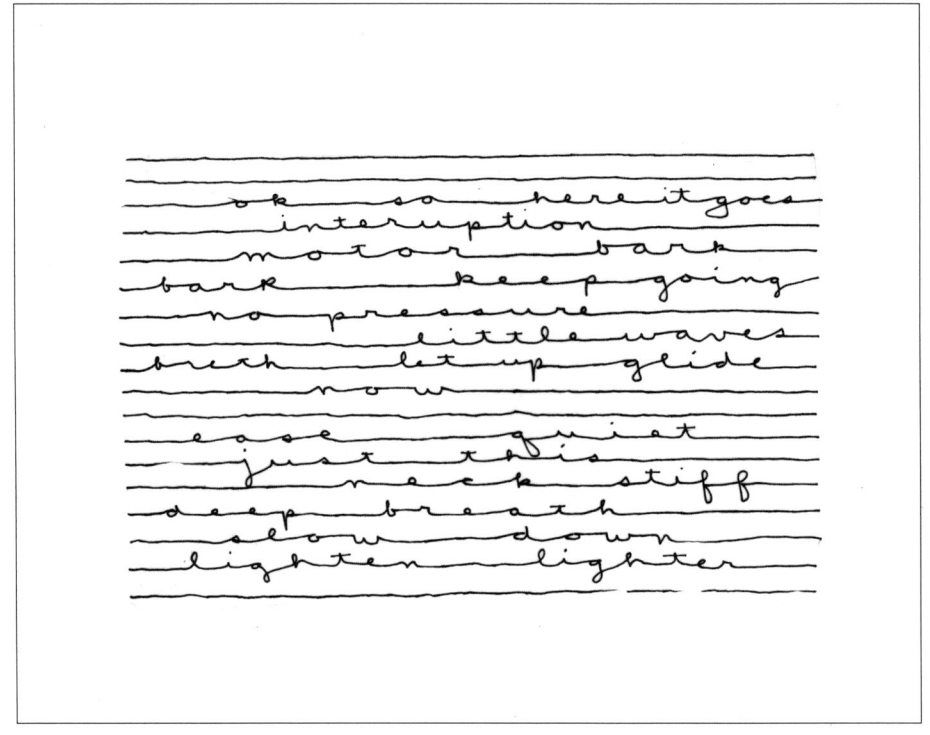

project 4

ALONG THESE LINES OF THOUGHT

mindfulness & acceptance

Most of us can observe our normal thinking processes to one degree or another. We see certain productive patterns of thought and other patterns that aren't so helpful. We know our minds often generate useless chatter, repetitious ruminations, invented storylines, and a variety of daydreams. We're often distracted by runaway thoughts when it might be better to focus on what is happening around us and what we're doing in the present moment.

If we examine the contents of our thoughts, we see they may contain valuable insights, but they don't always capture the complete picture. Our thoughts are often colored by positive or negative experiences from the past and shaped by future possibilities and concerns. A great deal of stress can occur when our thoughts are skewed. It's essential to remember that thoughts are only thoughts, not necessarily facts.

Fortunately, we can monitor and manage our thoughts to some extent. We can train our minds to become more aware, focused, fact-based, and calm through mindfulness and meditation practices.

It's important to note that not all types of meditation are helpful for all individuals. Some people who have experienced trauma may find that stressful memories, emotions, and flashbacks arise when practicing sitting meditation. A different, more active approach to meditation, such as tai chi, qigong, yoga, or walking meditation may be a better fit when beginning a practice.

Structured art and writing methods can also serve as forms of meditative and mindful practice. You'll experience one such method in this project when you create a simple artwork through drawing horizontal lines, briefly noting your thoughts as they arise, then refocusing your attention on horizontal line making. You'll experience your thoughts as they appear on the surface of the paper in much the same way as they pass through your mind. If you often have racing thoughts, you may notice that during this process your thoughts tend to slow down.

PREPARATIONS

- Clear and protect the surface of your artmaking table.
- Gather tools and materials: pencil and eraser
  9"x12" sheet of tracing paper, 1 sheet
  9"x12" white mixed media paper, 1 sheet
  black ultra-fine pen
  scissors
  glue stick

- Minimize noise and the potential for interruptions.
- If you experience a notable increase in your stress level while doing this project, take a break.
- As you follow directions, be curious and open to what occurs. Refrain from judging the correctness or quality of your artwork and writing.
- If it's comfortable to do so, close your eyes and consciously enjoy three breaths, being aware of the air moving through your nose or the subtle expansion and contraction of your diaphragm.
- Notice where your body is contacting the chair, floor, or table. Look around the room. Experience a sense of being present in your body and surroundings as you begin.

DIRECTIONS

step 1
Describe one thing that is pleasing to you in the room or something you see through a window if one is nearby.

_____

_____

_____

step 2
Cut a sheet of tracing paper in half. Orient it horizontally. With a pencil, lightly draw a border approximately ¾"- 1" inside all edges of the tracing paper. It's not necessary to measure the width of this border, imperfections often make artwork more interesting. Perfection is not a goal.

You'll be drawing horizontal lines and writing words inside this border.

step 3
While keeping your eyes on the ink tip of an ultra-fine pen, slowly draw one horizontal line from left to right over the topmost pencil line of the border. It's impossible to hand-draw a perfectly straight line, so don't be concerned about that. It's normal for your lines to look wobbly or shaky and you may also notice some ink blobs along the way.

step 4

Approximately ¼"- ½" down from the first line, slowly draw a second parallel line. Again, keep your eyes focused on the ink tip of the pen as you move from left to right across the paper without trying to make a perfectly straight line.

During this project you may experience stress, calmness, or even boredom. Don't judge your response to the artmaking process, just let it be as it is. If your stress level increases significantly, take a break.

step 5

Read the instructions in this step before continuing. View the artwork examples at the beginning of this project for a visual reference before you follow the artmaking steps.

As you continue to slowly move down the paper at approximately ¼"- ½" intervals, thoughts will naturally arise in your mind. Note the contents of these thoughts on the tracing paper by writing 1-3 words and then gently return your attention to the tip of the pen as it moves across the paper. Continue to slowly draw lines and briefly note your thoughts.

Don't judge or cling to your thoughts, just be aware of them and note them on the paper. Take the pen off the paper's surface only when you reach the right-hand border. Dot any *i*'s and cross any *t*'s as you return the pen to the left border to draw the next line.

If you notice you're gripping the pen tightly or pressing down hard on the tip, consciously release some of the pressure. You may need to pause and stretch your hand before beginning again.

Since you're writing slower than usual, your handwriting may appear elongated as it crosses the page. You may misspell words. That's a normal part of this process.

Stop making lines and writing thoughts when you're midway down the page.

step 6

Relax. Look around the room or through a nearby window. Describe something pleasant that's different from what you noticed in step 1.

_____

_____

_____

step 7

Stretch your writing hand. Gently move your arms and shoulders. Slowly continue to make lines and note your thoughts as they arise. Stop when you reach the bottom pencil line.

If you'd like, erase the pencil lines on the borders.

step 8
Put glue on the backside corners of the half-sheet tracing paper with your lines and words. Place your artwork in the center of a sheet of white mixed media paper.

step 9
Look at your artwork without judgment. Do you see more empty lines or more lines with writing?

Do your hand-drawn lines change in any way as they go down the paper?

Did your thoughts seem to slow down, speed up, or stay the same, compared to the usual speed of your thoughts in everyday life?

step 10
Silently read the words you wrote on the tracing paper. Without judgment, be curious about what you have written. Were your thoughts pleasant, unpleasant, or neutral? Did your thoughts relate to the past, present, or future?

Now read the words out loud as if they were a poem.

Following are two examples of poems from artmakers who have previously completed this project.

BIG LOVE

exile   lonely
why   shaky
saying goodbye   good wishes

heart
safeguard   chrysalis
wings
hope to see
someday   happened
hold
and
begin
big love

THINKING ABOUT THINKING

time to timeout   catch time
ticking   slow it   let it skim
the room   stay attached
shadow my hand

breathe the wing
airplane's buzz   dissolve into black
ink   inconsistent road   here
there   here

On a separate sheet of paper, use your words and phrases as they are or revise them to create a poem. What title would you give your poem?

Your writing may have a message for you. If so, write it below.

Feel free to spend time now or later to reflect on your words and phrases. The meaning of any artistic or creative endeavor may expand or change with additional contemplation.

LIFE APPLICATIONS

- As with any form of meditation, thoughts and emotions will naturally arise while you're meditating. The goal of meditation is not to stop thoughts, but to become aware of them and then gently return your focus to the practice.

- You may choose to do this project for a few days in a row as a daily meditation. You may decide to do this project on a routine basis. Over time you might find you're more adept at directing your awareness toward the present moment and your ability to focus your thoughts may also improve.

- During the day, pause occasionally to observe your thoughts:

  Be aware of what you're thinking.
  Accept your thoughts without judgment, whether they're pleasant, unpleasant, or neutral.
  Consider whether your thoughts are currently helpful or not.
  Remember that thoughts are only thoughts; they're not necessarily facts.
  Ask yourself if it makes sense to act on your thoughts.
  If not, gently refocus your attention on the present moment.
  Notice your surroundings and current sensory experiences and return to the task at hand.

CONCLUSIONS

- Note any useful insights, revelations, beliefs, or intentions that emerged while you worked on this project or that come to mind now.

  _____

  _____

  _____

- Detect any tension you're holding in your neck, shoulders, or elsewhere in your body. Consciously relax, pat, massage, or gently stretch those areas.
- If it's comfortable to do so, close your eyes and consciously enjoy three breaths.
- Notice where your body is contacting the chair, floor, or table. Look around the room. Experience a sense of being present in your body and surroundings as you finish.
- Sign and date your artwork. Store it for safekeeping.

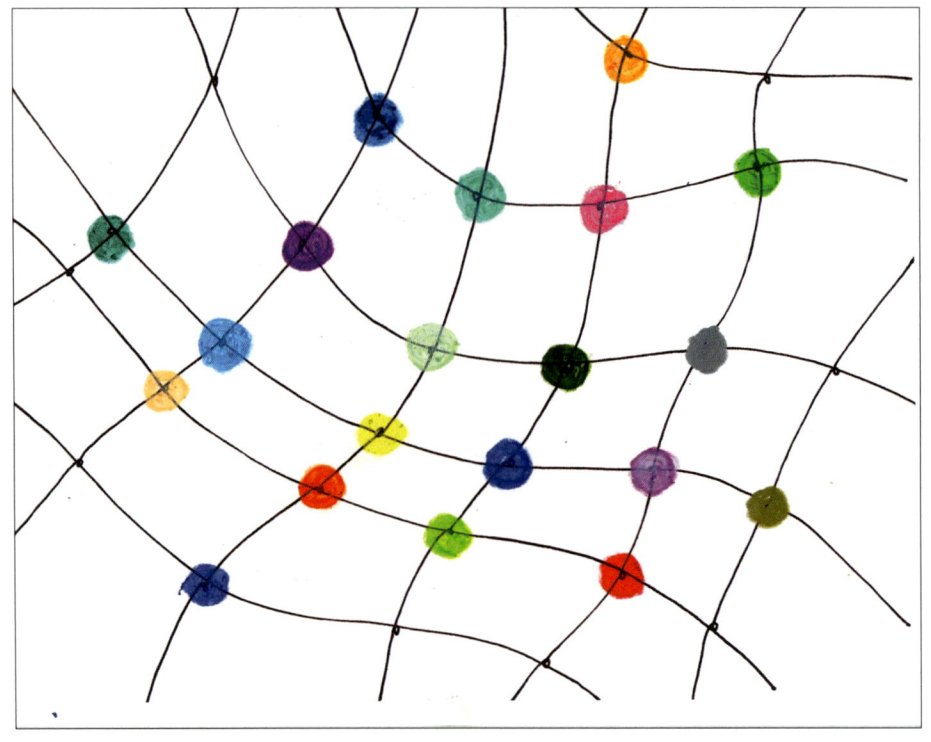

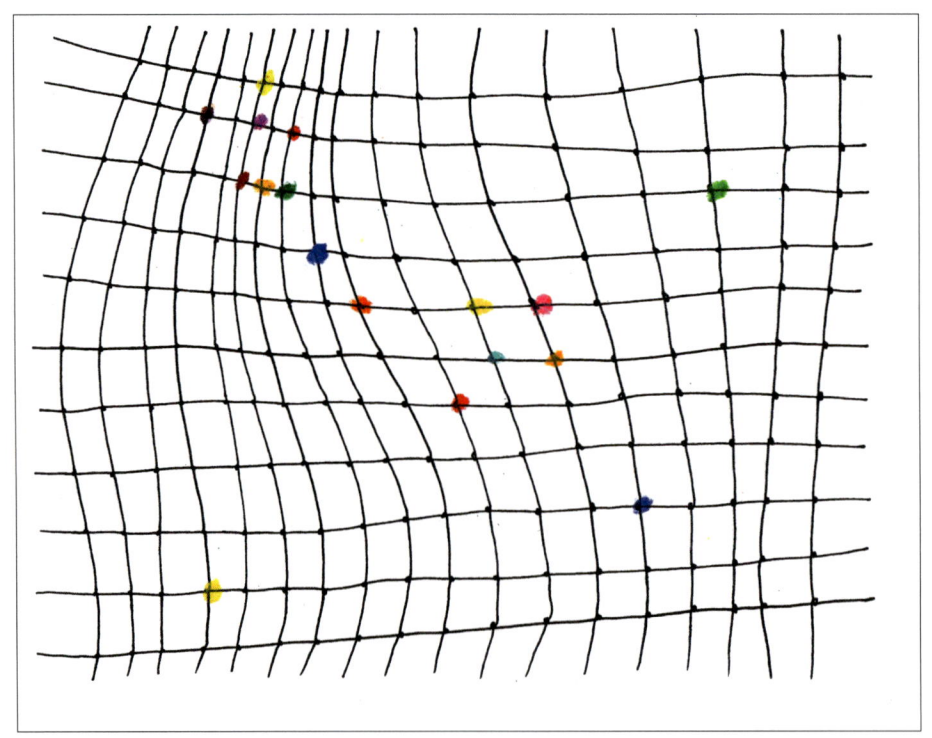

project 5

CAST AN EVER-WIDER NET

interconnections & reflections

Our basic needs are largely dependent on sources other than ourselves. We rely on rain, trees, and oceans to supply the oxygen we breathe, and we count on other natural resources, including the sun, to provide usable energy and raw materials. More than likely, other people grow our food, build our homes, and sew our clothing. Numerous interdependent connections crisscross our planet to sustain our lives.

With increased awareness of the interconnected nature of our lives, we realize each of us holds an influential place in the world. When we experience stress due to loneliness, disempowerment, or perceived insignificance, we can remind ourselves that we're a valuable part of a far-reaching network.

This project focuses on connections among people and how our choices in life not only affect ourselves and others but also the world. To illustrate these connections, a metaphoric legend called *Indra's Net* is brought into play.

In this legend, jewels are fastened to the loops or knots that hold a net together. These jewels reflect light across the universe. A single act or thought, whether it's one of goodwill or ill-intent will ripple across the net to the farthest reaches. Each one of us is a jewel on the net, actively participating in the evolution of our world.

To represent the give-and-take of connections, you'll begin by choosing one of the provided net drawings or you can opt to draw a net of your own creation. Using oil pastels, you'll color in several "jewels" to symbolize yourself, friends, family, and supports, as well as other interconnections that are nearby and perhaps a few that are farther away. Prompts are provided for you to write a simple ode, which is a poem of praise or appreciation.

PREPARATIONS

- Clear and protect the surface of your artmaking table.
- Gather tools and materials: pen or pencil for writing
  black ultra-fine pen
  oil pastels
  scissors
  glue stick
  9"x12" white mixed media paper, 1 sheet

- Minimize noise and the potential for interruptions.
- You may opt to work on this project in more than one sitting.
- If you experience a notable increase in your stress level while doing this project, take a break.
- As you follow directions, be curious and open to what occurs. Refrain from judging the correctness or quality of your artwork and writing.
- If it's comfortable to do so, close your eyes and consciously enjoy three breaths, being aware of the air moving through your nose or the subtle expansion and contraction of your diaphragm.
- Notice where your body is contacting the chair, floor, or table. Look around the room. Experience a sense of being present in your body and surroundings as you begin.

DIRECTIONS

step 1

Imagine the numerous connections among people involved in providing food to sustain your physical body—people who plant, water, harvest, transport, and display food for you to buy in markets. Consider the interconnections you have with healthcare providers, such as doctors, nurses, technicians, physical therapists, pharmacists, dentists, and eye doctors who help to maintain your physical body.

Think about people who construct houses and those who connect water, electricity, and gas to your living space so you're protected from the elements and live in relative comfort. Take account of all the people who picked the cotton, wove the fabric, sewed the garments, stitched the shoes, and sold the articles of clothing you're wearing today that keep you warm and dry.

List a few interconnected worker-providers that are important to you.

step 2
List people who are close to you, such as friends, family, partners, acquaintances, as well as pets and others who play social and supportive roles in your life.

_____

_____

_____

_____

_____

step 3
There may be people you have never met in person who inspire you. List them below.

_____

_____

_____

_____

_____

step 4
List any groups or organizations you belong to that provide you with a sense of connection.

_____

_____

_____

_____

_____

step 5
Are there family members, friends, partners, acquaintances, other people, organizations, or pets you provide support to? If so, list them below.

_____

_____

_____

_____

_____

_____

step 6
Select and remove one of the following net image pages. If you want to use the provided net images more than once, feel free to trace or photocopy them. Alternatively, draw a net image of your own design on a sheet of mixed media paper.

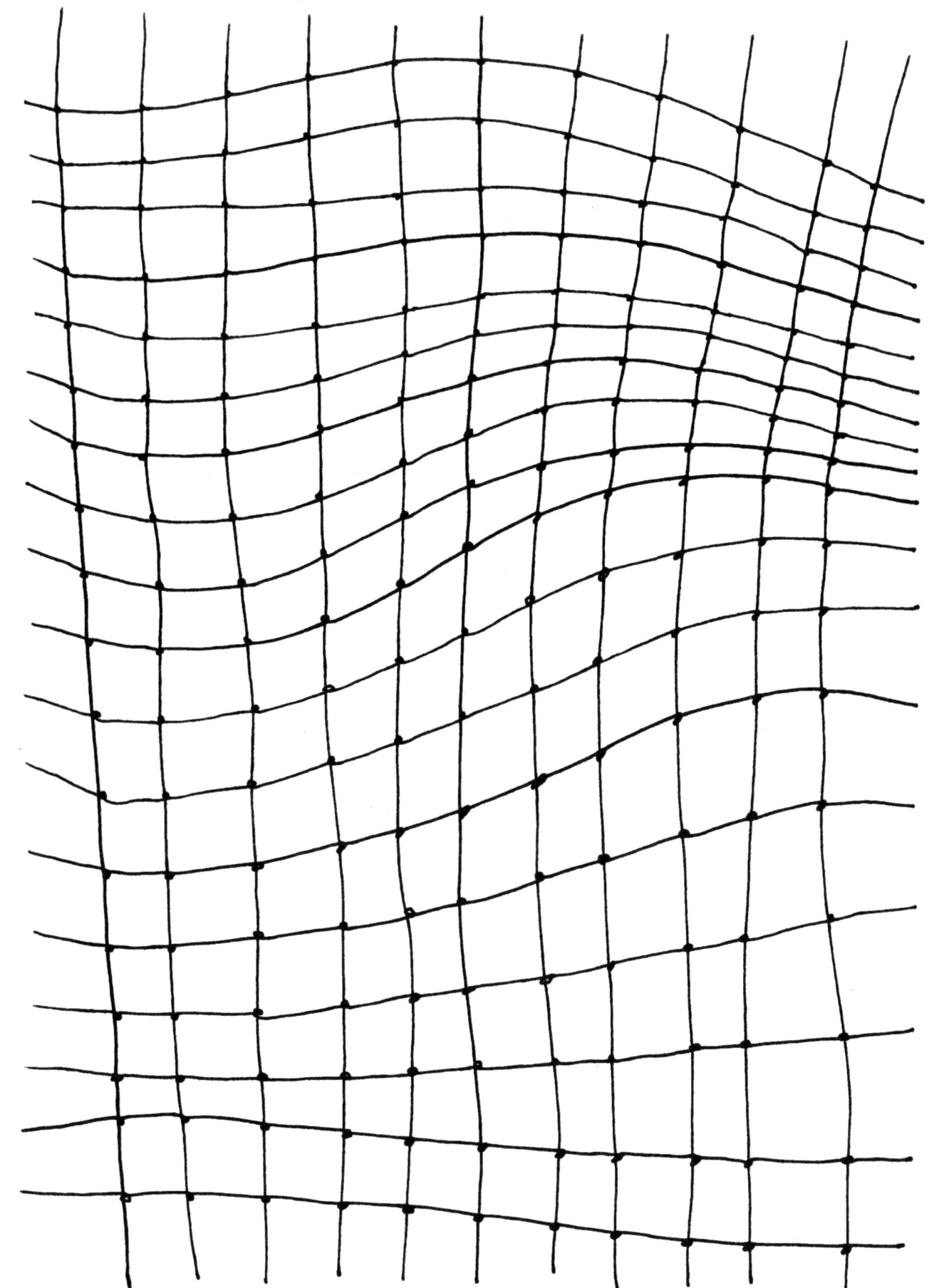

step 7

Choose an oil pastel color to represent yourself. What color is it? _____
Color in a dot or circle at a centrally located intersection on the net you selected.

step 8

Look over the lists you made in steps 1-5. Circle some of the people or groups you'd like to include on your net. Choose an oil pastel color for each one you circled and place a dab of that color next to the name of each person or group, so you'll know which color represents that person or group.

Color a dot or circle at an intersection on the net to represent each person or group you circled. You may want to start at the center of the net with people closest to you such as family or friends and move outward toward the edges. You can also place a dot or two for other people whose names you don't know, but who provide you with a sense of human connection.

You don't need to color all the intersections with dots. When you're finished coloring dots or circles, apply glue to the backside corners of your net. Glue it to the middle of a sheet of white mixed media paper.

step 9

Look at your artwork from a distance. Imagine the colored dots or circles are jewels fastened to the network of your current life. Imagine how each one reflects or shines light throughout the world.

step 10

In this step you'll be writing an ode in praise or appreciation of one of the following:

- the concept of interdependent connection
- an interlinked chain or category of people, such as food supply workers or healthcare providers
- friends, family members, or supportive groups
- one specific friend, family member, pet, or group

Following are four examples of odes written by artmakers who previously completed this project.

ODE TO INTERCONNECTIONS

From many directions, infinite
glints of multifaceted exchange
undulate across the universe,
linking and looping their way
to reflect through my mind's eye,
versed in words of worthy offering.

ODE TO OUR DAILY SAVIORS

Oh, how you field the plows, furrow the seeds,
sprout the soil, rain the leaves, sun the plants,
vine the stakes, stalk the corn, pod the peas,
truck the pickings, shell the beans, can the beets,
label the goodness, deliver the goods, fruit the shelves.

Oh, how we season the convenience, feast the flavors,
enjoy the chew, savor the sustenance,
swallow your toil, and consume the goodness.

ODE TO HOLDING AND BEING HELD

A sight to behold.
Sapphire blue radiates from my mother.
A brother will not let me drown.
Friends place amethysts in my hand.
Giving shelter to my wounds.
Gratitude for the gifts.
Facets in the light.
Give and take.
Remember the net woven for me.
Be a strong rope in the net for others.
Hold each other tight.
Joined together for all time.

ODE TO MY BEST FRIEND

Thanks for all the good times, the adventures,
the laughter, the crazy dances we invented.
Thanks for being there when I needed you,
for offering me advice to keep me going.
Thanks for being who you are everyday
and always.

Circle any of the following words or phrases you might like to include in your writing.

gemstones	jewels	crystals	brightness	sparkle	brilliance	glittering
gratitude	stars	reflections	multifaceted	treasure	infinite	glints
cross-connect	joined	give & take	survival	nourish	reciprocal	link
one and all	network	back & forth	collaboration	support	reliance	knotted
safety net	alliance	mutual	cooperation	exchange	protection	praise
sustenance	flow	shelter	kindred	bonds	conjunction	looped
tie-ins	interacting	comfort	allies	relationship	juncture	entwined
attachments	world	planet	sun	moon	ripple	undulate

in all directions   sight to behold   twinkling of an eye   cast a wide net
today's catch   infinite net worth   interconnected networks   each jewel reflects all jewels

amethyst: violet, purple   emerald: green   topaz: various colors   ruby: deep red
garnet: red   sapphire: blue   aquamarine: blue-green   diamond: clear, blue, yellow, pink
citrine: deep gold yellow   peridot: olive, lime

Write your ode below. When you're finished writing, enjoy reading it out loud so you can both hear and see it. Give your ode a title.

_____ (title) _____

_____

_____

_____

_____

_____

_____

LIFE APPLICATIONS

- What is one small choice you can make now that may have a positive effect on you, as well as a positive ripple effect on others and the world?

- Is there someone you would like to personally thank who you included in your net? If so, why, how, and when will you do this?

- It's good to be grateful for the connections we already have in our lives, but sometimes we may want to add an individual or group or grow closer to someone. What is one way you would like to alter your network? Will this change help to reduce your stress or invigorate your life? How will you work toward this change?

- You can revisit your art and writing from this project if their messages and insights are beneficial to you. Feel free to do this project more than once.

CONCLUSIONS

- Note any useful insights, revelations, beliefs, or intentions that emerged while you worked on this project or that come to mind now.

- Detect any tension you're holding in your neck, shoulders, or elsewhere in your body. Consciously relax, pat, massage, or gently stretch those areas.
- If it's comfortable to do so, close your eyes and consciously enjoy three breaths.
- Notice where your body is contacting the chair, floor, or table. Look around the room. Experience a sense of being present in your body and surroundings as you finish.
- Sign and date your artwork. Store it for safekeeping.

project 6

READ MOTION INTO EMOTION

description & imagination

To be fully alive and safe, we need to feel all our emotions. Accepting and working with our emotions as they arise helps us to better understand ourselves and respond to situations and other people in more effective ways. Seeing our emotions as normal, helpful, and informative can provide insight and direction in our daily lives, thereby lowering our stress.

Since anxiety, anger, fear, and sadness may alert us to potential danger or the need to attend to something crucial in our lives, these emotions are essential for our personal survival as well as the survival of our species.

To protect us, a so-called negativity bias has been hardwired into our brains over hundreds of thousands of years with the result that we often pay more attention to unpleasant feelings as compared to pleasant ones. Consequently, we need to acknowledge our positive feelings more often and make extra efforts to create and enjoy experiences that make us feel contented or happy.

With increased awareness of the ever-changing nature of our emotions and our ability to experience both pleasant and unpleasant feelings within a short time span, we can learn to feel all our emotions without becoming overly reactive or excessively attached to them. We can let them be as they are, respond if necessary, and then let them go as they naturally pass through our minds and bodies.

In this project, you'll combine two abstract line drawings: one representing pleasant emotions and one representing unpleasant emotions. You'll imagine how these lines might move if they become animated. You'll write creative descriptions of these motions on your artwork by selecting words from provided lists.

PREPARATIONS

- Clear and protect the surface of your artmaking table.
- Gather tools and materials: pen or pencil for writing
  - black ultra-fine pen
  - black chisel-tip marker
  - white scrap paper
  - 9"x12" tracing paper, 1 sheet
  - 9"x12" white mixed media paper, 1 sheet
  - scissors
  - glue stick
  - white oil pastel

- Minimize noise and the potential for interruptions.
- You may opt to work on this project in more than one sitting.
- If you experience a notable increase in your stress level while doing this project, take a break.
- As you follow directions, be curious and open to what occurs. Refrain from judging the correctness or quality of your artwork and writing.
- If it's comfortable to do so, close your eyes and consciously enjoy three breaths, being aware of the air moving through your nose or the expansion and contraction of your diaphragm.
- Notice where your body is contacting the chair, floor, or table. Look around the room. Experience a sense of being present in your body and surroundings as you begin.

DIRECTIONS

step 1
On white scrap paper, draw each of the following types of lines using both an ultra-fine pen and chisel-tip marker. Your lines may or may not overlap one another.

straight lines: vertical, horizontal, diagonal
curved lines: half-moon, wavy, looped, spiral
other lines: zigzag, dots, dashes, scribbling

step 2
Briefly note one pleasant experience that occurred today or in the past couple of days. It could be something simple, such as light coming through a window, a bird chirping, drinking a cup of tea, or smelling a ripe peach at the grocery store. It might be playing a sport or game, enjoying the company of a friend, going for a walk, or playing with a pet.

_____

_____

In your body, where do you feel the pleasant emotions associated with this experience? _____

Cut a sheet of tracing paper in half. Look at the examples of lines you drew on scrap paper in step 1. Choose 2-3 of these types of lines that can represent how you felt during or after this pleasant experience.

Use an ultra-fine pen and/or chisel-tip marker to draw these lines on a half-sheet of tracing paper. You may want to enlarge or decrease the size of the lines you drew on scrap paper or change their shape. You can repeat types of lines, group them together, keep them separate, or overlap them. Your abstract line drawing may be minimal or more complex.

step 3

Look at your line drawing. Circle words from the following list that metaphorically describe these lines.

DOT: morsel   particle   point   speck   drop   twinkle   tick   sprinkle   sparkle   glitter   rash   grain   gnat

DASH/SHORT LINE: spurt   sprint   link   zing   glint   hyphen   splinter   dribble   broken arrow

STRAIGHT LINE: stick   ray   bar   stream   mast   bridge   furrow   post   outpost   stripe   seam   road   rod   beam   street   horizon   walkway

CURVED LINE: wave   loop   ribbon   stream   curlicue   coil   spring   undulation   arch   arc   billow   stem   hill   whorl   crescent   slinky   bow   slope   rope   dip   flounce   ruffle   snake   bump   stroke   curl   path   river   spiral   band   ripple

SLANTED LINE: slash   ramp   lean-to   oblique   skew   catty-corner   glancing   shaft   tilt   tangent   bevel

ANGULAR LINE: jag   zigzag   rickrack   bolt   thorn   barbed-wire   spike   corner   cone   fissure   contortion   peak   ridge   ricochet   bend   akimbo   switchback   crack   crevice

SCRIBBLED LINE: hassle   gnarl   knot   jumble   melee   tangle   mumbo-jumbo   stew   hurly-burly   heap   blizzard   quagmire   mishmash

THIN/LIGHT LINE: filament   tendril   strand   string   thread   fiber   wire   effervescence   breeze   frolic   whim   vapor   wind   wisp   trace   trifle   vapor trail

THICK/HEAVY LINE: chunk   reinforcement   girder   brace   cable   twine   cord   rope   pole

Imagine how your drawn lines would move if they became animated. Circle words to describe the movement of each type of line.

SLOW: crawl   creep   amble   dawdle   lope   stagger   shuffle   flounder   slink   trudge   traipse   slither   waddle   waver   limp   stroll   float   drift   tiptoe   sway   wobble   roam   rove   wander   falter   glide

MEDIUM SPEED: hop   prance   promenade   sashay   sail   scamper   scramble   scoot   march   skip   slide   soar   strut   canter   trot   jump   rock   jaunt   sprint   spurt   twirl   flow   jitter   swoop   flail   stride   bob-up   bob-down   walk   swim   skid   lurch

FAST: chase   dart   dash   dive   gallop   hurl   hurry   propel   race   run   rush   scurry   speed   spin   spring   sprint   skitter   streak   swerve   swing   snap   whisk   zip   zoom   zap   plummet   thrash   swat   plunge   shove   smash   stomp   surge   gush   crash   leap   lunge   slam   nab   pounce   snatch   trounce

VARIOUS SPEEDS: careen   pivot   swivel   oscillate   undulate   vibrate   quiver   twitch   fluctuate   roll   kick   vacillate   teeter-totter   wiggle   bounce   writhe   twist   fly   sweep   climb   fall   flap   reel   pour   tremble   shiver   blow   bump   collide   jab   jerk   scrawl   skim   tumble   drive   dance

Circle 1-3 words below that describe your feelings during or following the pleasant experience you described in step 2.

happy	delighted	amazed	bliss	contented	serene	thankful	inspired
amused	excited	joyful	ecstatic	calm	peaceful	mellow	positive
upbeat	cheerful	proud	euphoric	satisfied	pleased	surprised	good

step 4

Write 1-3 phrases combining some or all the words you wrote in step 2 and circled in step 3. You may want to change the form or order of the words or add more words.

Following are examples of phrases written by artmakers who previously completed this project:

looped ribbons sashay through my mind   *soaring twirling joyful monarch*

calm rays of light glitter through air   *undulating hurly-burly takes a leap*

_____

_____

Using an ultra-fine pen and/or chisel-tip marker, write or print one or more of your phrases on your artwork following the direction of lines, across lines, or on top of lines. Another alternative would be to write them toward the edges of the tracing paper. Your writing can be large, small, or a mixture of both.

step 5

Note one unpleasant stressful experience that occurred today or in the past couple of days.

_____

_____

Where do you sense this unpleasant experience in your body? _____

Look at the examples of lines you drew on scrap paper. Choose 2-3 of these types of lines that can represent how you felt during or after this unpleasant experience.

Use an ultra-fine pen and/or chisel-tip marker to draw these lines on a second half-sheet of tracing paper. You may want to enlarge or decrease the size of the lines you drew on scrap paper or change the shape. You can repeat types of lines, group them together, keep them separate, or overlap them. Your abstract line drawing may be minimal or more complex.

step 6

Look at this second line drawing. Circle words that metaphorically describe the lines you drew.

DOT: morsel   particle   point   speck   drop   twinkle   tick   sprinkle   sparkle   glitter   rash   grain   gnat

DASH/SHORT LINE: spurt   sprint   link   zing   glint   hyphen   splinter   dribble   broken arrow

STRAIGHT LINE: stick   ray   bar   stream   mast   bridge   furrow   post   outpost   stripe   seam   road   rod   beam   street   horizon   walkway

CURVED LINE: wave   loop   ribbon   stream   curlicue   coil   spring   undulation   arch   arc   billow   stem   hill   whorl   crescent   slinky   bow   slope   rope   dip   flounce   ruffle   snake   bump   stroke   curl   path   river   spiral   band   ripple

SLANTED LINE: slash   ramp   lean-to   oblique   skew   catty-corner   glancing   shaft   tilt   tangent   bevel

ANGULAR LINE: jag   zigzag   rick-rack   bolt   thorn   barbed-wire   spike   corner   cone   fissure   contortion   peak   ridge   ricochet   bend   akimbo   switchback   crack   crevice

SCRIBBLED LINE: hassle   gnarl   knot   jumble   melee   tangle   mumbo-jumbo   stew   hurly-burley   heap   blizzard   quagmire   mishmash

THIN/LIGHT LINE: filament   tendril   strand   string   thread   fiber   wire   effervescence   breeze   frolic   whim   vapor   wind   wisp   trace   trifle   vapor trail

THICK/HEAVY LINE: chunk   reinforcement   girder   brace   cable   twine   cord   rope   pole

Imagine how your drawn lines would move if they became animated. Circle words to describe the movement of each type of line.

SLOW: crawl   creep   amble   dawdle   lope   stagger   shuffle   flounder   slink   trudge   traipse   slither   waddle   waver   limp   stroll   float   drift   tiptoe   sway   wobble   roam   rove   wander   falter   glide

MEDIUM SPEED: hop   prance   promenade   sashay   sail   scamper   scramble   scoot   march   skip   slide   soar   strut   canter   trot   jump   rock   jaunt   sprint   spurt   twirl   flow   jitter   swoop   flail   stride   bob-up   bob-down   walk   swim   skid   lurch   squirm

FAST: chase   dart   dash   dive   gallop   hurl   hurry   propel   race   run   rush   scurry   speed   spin   spring   sprint   skitter   streak   swerve   swing   snap   whisk   zip   zoom   zap   plummet   thrash   swat   plunge   shove   smash   stomp   surge   gush   crash   leap   lunge   slam   nab   pounce   snatch   trounce

VARIOUS SPEEDS: careen   pivot   swivel   oscillate   undulate   vibrate   quiver   twitch   fluctuate   roll   kick   vacillate   teeter-totter   wiggle   bounce   writhe   twist   fly   sweep   climb   fall   flap   reel   pour   tremble   shiver   blow   bump   collide   jab   jerk   scrawl   skim   tumble   drive   dance

Circle 1-3 words below that describe your feelings during or following your unpleasant experience.

sad	melancholic	ashamed	dread	threatened	irritated	rageful
lonely	hurt	remorseful	suspicious	alarmed	frustrated	rebellious
forlorn	grief-stricken	fearful	doubtful	horrified	aggravated	jealous
gloomy	sorrowful	nervous	cautious	angry	furious	resentful
disappointed	heartbroken	anxious	frightened	annoyed	hateful	disgusted

step 7

Write 1-3 phrases combining some or all the words you wrote in step 5 and circled in step 6. You may want to change the form or order of the words and add more words.

Following are examples of phrases written by artmakers who have previously completed this project.

remorseful questions careen and race   *a quagmire of threads squirm with doubt*

anger streaks through the moment   *rickrack contorts then plummets into sadness*

_____

_____

_____

Using an ultra-fine pen and/or chisel-tip marker, write or print one or more of your phrases on your artwork. Your writing can be large, small, or a mixture of both.

For both artworks, read your written phrases out loud so you can see and hear what you have written.

step 8

Create a collage by combining your two tracing paper artworks on a sheet of white mixed media paper. You may put them side-by-side, on top of each other, or overlap them. You may also cut or tear the artworks. Once you have decided on a meaningful arrangement, glue it to the white paper. Note the significance of the arrangement.

_____

_____

step 9

If you want, you can lightly color white oil pastel over some of the black lines or writing on your artwork to represent how emotions fade and pass through your body and mind with time.

step 10

Look at your artwork from a distance. What is it like to see your emotions on a piece of paper in black and white, instead of experiencing them inside your body and mind?

_____

What is it like to see and read about your unpleasant emotions along with your pleasant emotions? Can you hold both in your mind at once? If so, what is a positive effect of doing this?

_____

_____

Give your artwork a title: _____

LIFE APPLICATIONS

- Emotion check-ins can reduce your overall stress load. A simple and quick way to check-in is to ask yourself whether you're feeling sad, glad, mad, or neutral. By naming your emotions more precisely, you're able to make better decisions about how to respond to them. Use the list below to identify your emotions more specifically.

happy	contented	sad	surprised	angry
amused	calm	lonely	fearful	annoyed
upbeat	satisfied	forlorn	nervous	irritated
delighted	serene	gloomy	anxious	frustrated
excited	peaceful	disappointed	dread	aggravated
cheerful	pleased	melancholic	suspicious	furious
amazed	thankful	hurt	doubtful	hateful
joyful	mellow	grief-stricken	cautious	rageful
proud	unemotional	sorrowful	frightened	rebellious
blissful	indifferent	heartbroken	threatened	jealous
ecstatic	numb	ashamed	alarmed	resentful
euphoric	bored	remorseful	horrified	disgusted

Emotional states can be complex. More than one word may be needed to describe your emotional state at any given time. Keep in mind that a single event or situation can initiate both pleasant and unpleasant emotions simultaneously.

- When experiencing intense emotions, determine which one or more of the following responses will serve you best.

    1. Accept and be with my emotions.
    2. Allow them to naturally dissipate.
    3. Change my focus of attention through distraction.
    4. Obtain more facts.
    5. Act safely and appropriately on my emotions.

- Sometimes we identify so strongly with our emotions, we believe we are our emotions. To avoid this, instead of thinking or saying, "I am sad," you can say or think, "I feel sad."

CONCLUSIONS

- Note any useful insights, revelations, beliefs, or intentions that emerged while you worked on this project or that come to mind now.

_____

_____

- Detect any tension you're holding in your neck, shoulders, or elsewhere in your body. Consciously relax, pat, massage, or gently stretch those areas.
- If it's comfortable to do so, close your eyes and consciously enjoy three breaths.
- Notice where your body is contacting the chair, floor, or table. Look around the room. Experience a sense of being present in your body and surroundings as you finish.
- Sign and date your artwork. Store it for safekeeping.

project 7

SENSORY AWARENESS DIPTYCH

relaxation & regeneration

Each moment of our lives is unique. This moment has never happened before and will never happen again. Even when we're in a familiar environment doing routine tasks, the multi-sensory possibilities that surround us are impossible to exactly duplicate.

Our senses provide the most direct connection we have with the world, yet often we're not fully aware of all the sounds, smells, tastes, textures, and sights available to us. With increased awareness, we can be more open to receiving sensory cues from our environment, allowing us to gather vital information, experience life more fully, be safe, and reduce stress.

Of course, not all sensory experiences are pleasant, some are neutral or even offensive; it all depends on how we interpret the information that enters our brains through our ears, noses, tongues, skin, and eyes. What is tasty or beautiful to one person may be sickening or ugly to another. In any case, we can be more open to receive sensory experiences as messages or gifts and seek out sounds, smells, textures, tastes, and visuals that inspire, soothe, and energize us.

Descriptions of two breathing techniques are provided to help you soothe or energize, depending on your wants and needs.

You'll create two miniature abstract artworks to make a diptych (two artworks placed side-by-side), then write two descriptions to set the scenes for a soothing environment and an energizing one.

PREPARATIONS

- Clear and protect the surface of your artmaking table.
- Gather tools and materials: pen or pencil for writing
  scissors
  glue stick
  white scrap paper
  9"x12" mixed media paper, 2 sheets
  oil pastels
  paper towel

- Minimize noise and the potential for interruptions.
- You can opt to work on this project in more than one sitting.
- If you experience a notable increase in your stress level while doing this project, take a break.
- As you follow directions, be curious and open to what occurs. Refrain from judging the correctness or quality of your artwork and writing.
- If it's comfortable to do so, close your eyes and consciously enjoy three breaths, being aware of the air moving through your nose or the expansion and contraction of your diaphragm.
- Notice where your body is contacting the chair, floor, or table. Look around the room. Experience a sense of being present in your body and surroundings as you begin.

DIRECTIONS

step 1
Note 3-5 sounds or types of music that soothe you.

_____

_____

_____

Note 3-5 sounds or types of music that energize you.

_____

_____

_____

step 2
From the list below or from other smells that come to mind, what are 3-5 smells that soothe you?

vanilla	jasmine	sandalwood	bergamot	black tea	basil	sweet orange
lemon	curry	chocolate	lavender	rosemary	mint	eucalyptus
woods	grass	fresh air	coconut	coffee	rain	ocean
pine	rose	ginger	clove	cinnamon	lilac	gardenia

From the list above, or from what comes to mind, what are 3-5 smells that energize you?

step 3
From the list below or from other tastes that come to mind, what are 3-5 tastes that soothe you?

sour	tangy	creamy	coffee	herbs	nuts	ice cream
sweet	spicy	starchy	tea	fruit	lemon	meat
salty	fruity	buttery	chocolate	berries	bread	fish
bitter	savory	peppery	vegetables	banana	cheese	pickles

From the list above or from what comes to mind, what are 3-5 tastes that energize you?

step 4
From the list below or from other textures that come to mind, what are 3-5 textures that soothe you?

fur	velvet	cashmere	plastic	clay	leaf	wood
silk	fleece	linen	stone	grass	metal	dirt
wool	cotton	rock	water	sand	paper	feather
glass	shell	bark	bubbles	satin	marble	carpet

From the list above or from other textures that come to mind, note 3-5 textures that energize you.

step 5

What specific colors have a soothing effect on you? Are they pale, medium, deep, or bright shades?

_____

What specific colors have an energizing effect on you? Are they pale, medium, deep, or bright shades?

_____

step 6

In this step, you'll be experimenting with oil pastels on white scrap paper. Notice whether any of your oil pastels have picked up other colors. If so, wipe them with a small piece of clean paper towel. Don't hesitate to break your oil pastels in half. It can be easier to color with a shorter side of an oil pastel.

1. With any medium shade, use the end of an oil pastel to draw two lines: one using heavy pressure and the other using light pressure.

    Smear half of each line using a small piece of clean paper towel.

2. Use the side of a different medium shade oil pastel to apply a small swatch of color on the paper. Smudge the color with a small piece of clean paper towel.

    Use the side of a lighter or darker oil pastel on top of the color you just smudged.

3. Apply a layer of white oil pastel over another small area of the paper. Apply a layer of light color over that. Apply a third layer of white on top.

4. Apply a layer of a dark color over a small area of the paper. Apply a lighter color on top.

5. With yet another color, scribble over a small area of the paper without covering all the white background. Use a different oil pastel to color in any visible white background showing through. Smudge the colors with a small piece of clean paper towel.

step 7

Cut a sheet of white mixed media paper into four equal quarters.

On one quarter-sheet, create an abstract artwork with oil pastels using one or more soothing colors. You can use the end and/or side of oil pastels to make lines and shapes. If colors look too strong, remove some of the color with a small clean piece of paper towel or add white oil pastel to lighten the color. If you wish, you can blend and smooth colors with a small clean piece of paper towel.

step 8

On a second quarter-sheet of white mixed media paper, create an abstract artwork using energizing colors. You can use the end and/or side of an oil pastel to make lines and fill in areas or shapes. You may want to blend and smooth colors with a small clean piece of paper towel.

step 9

Center both artworks, side-by-side, on a sheet of white mixed media paper. Glue them to the white background to create a diptych.

Look at your diptych from arm's length. In this moment, would you rather be soothed or energized? Which side appeals to you more?

_____

Title your artwork: _____

step 10

You'll use some or all the soothing words you wrote in steps 1-5 as you imagine being in a soothing indoor or outdoor scene. Where are you? What is the temperature or weather like? What do you see, hear, smell, and touch in this environment?

Following is one example of writing from an artmaker who previously completed this project.

> *Feathers flutter in the breeze falling to pillow the sweet ripe peaches and apricots on the ground for easy eating. A kitten purrs, lapping warm milk and licking butter from my fingers. Its fur is as soft as peony petals. We nap together in the sun surrounded by lilac bushes and wake to the sound of chirping birds.*

Based on soothing words you circled or wrote in steps 1-5, write your description of a soothing scene on the blank lines below. Feel free to add any other soothing words or phrases that come to mind.

_____

_____

_____

_____

_____

_____

_____

Read your writing out loud so you can both see and hear your words.

step 11

You'll use some or all the energizing words you circled or wrote in steps 1-5 to describe an indoor or outdoor scene that is energizing to you. Where are you? What is the temperature or weather like? What do you see, hear, smell, and touch in this environment? Are there energizing activities available to you? Are you with other people?

Following is one example of writing from an artmaker who previously completed this project.

> *The table is set with red-orange plates and bright blue water glasses. As we enter the room, I see bowls of chili smothered in cheese. Ice cubes in a pitcher of limes and lemonade clink together as it is placed on the checkered tablecloth. A mariachi band is roaming around the room. The music is coming this way. There is much laughter and people are wildly waving their arms to the beat of the music.*

Based on the energizing words you wrote in steps 1-5, write your description of an energizing scene below. Feel free to add other energizing words or phrases that come to mind.

_____
_____
_____
_____
_____
_____
_____
_____

Read your writing out loud so you can both see and hear your words.

LIFE APPLICATIONS

- Throughout the day, take a moment to notice sounds, smells, textures, tastes, colors, and the quality of light in your immediate environment.

- Display objects that provide soothing and energizing sensory experiences for you. Some objects may provide more than one sensory experience such as a smooth stone or shell that you can see and touch or a bell that you can see, touch, and hear. Place these items in prominent locations so you can easily access them to soothe or energize. You can also place small objects in your car or workplace.

- If certain pleasant sensory experiences are currently unavailable to you, you can bring them to mind through your imagination. You can also recall the scenes you created in steps 10 and 11. Close your eyes to allow a more detailed, vivid version in your imagination.

- Depending on whether you need to soothe or energize, practice one of the breathing exercises below if it's comfortable for you to do so.

    BREATHING PRACTICE TO SOOTHE: Inhale fully through your nose. Exhale slowly and fully through your mouth with pursed lips. Repeat 1-3 times.

    BREATHING PRACTICE TO ENERGIZE: Stand straight with hands touching your shoulders, fingers curled slightly. As you rapidly inhale through your nose, raise your arms straight up. As you rapidly exhale, lower your arms with hands at shoulders. Repeat 6-8 times. Close your eyes. Relax for a moment.

- You can revisit your art and writing from this project if their messages and insights can be of benefit to you. Repeat this project whenever you wish.

CONCLUSIONS

- Note any useful insights, revelations, beliefs, or intentions that emerged while you worked on this project or that come to mind now.

_____

_____

_____

- Detect any tension you're holding in your neck, shoulders, or elsewhere in your body. Consciously relax, pat, massage, or gently stretch those areas.
- If it's comfortable to do so, close your eyes and consciously enjoy three breaths.
- Notice where your body is contacting the chair, floor, or table. Look around the room. Experience a sense of being present in your body and surroundings as you finish.
- Sign and date your artwork. Store it for safekeeping.

project **8**

WABI-SABI SENSE-OF-SELF

imperfection & authenticity

Stress can originate from a perceived need to be perfect, to successfully complete all our goals on schedule, or to fit into an ideal mold that we think will make us feel well-liked and happy.

To consider a different, less stressful point of view, we can turn to the time-honored art and philosophy of wabi-sabi that originated in Japan in the 15th century. It's based on appreciation for the hidden beauty of imperfection, impermanence, and incompleteness. Wabi-sabi aesthetics include asymmetry, earthiness, authenticity, and uniqueness. When looking at a wabi-sabi bowl or cup, many irregularities are apparent including blotches, cracks, uneven glaze, and an assortment of other flaws. These imperfections give wabi-sabi objects their one-of-a-kind characteristics.

When looking at ourselves through the aesthetics of wabi-sabi, we acknowledge our own imperfections, impermanence, and incompleteness, along with our hidden beauty. Whether we came by our imperfections through circumstances beyond our control or acquired them through our own actions, they teach us what it's like to be fully human. Our imperfections also help us understand, accept, and appreciate differences and imperfections in others.

To look at the hidden beauty and poetics of your own imperfections, as well as the effects of self-repair and self-renewal, you'll gather five different found or recycled papers to create a two-dimensional wabi-sabi bowl or cup. From your descriptions of the papers, you'll write a Tanka poem, which is a short five-line classical form of Japanese poetry based on syllable count.

PREPARATIONS

- Clear and protect the surface of your artmaking table.
- Gather tools and materials: pencil and eraser
  black ultra-fine pen
  black chisel-tip marker
  scissors
  glue stick
  9"x12" white mixed media paper, 1 sheet
  found or recycled papers, such as used bags, maps, envelopes, notebook pads, wrapping and artist's papers, waste papers, or any paper product that will adhere with a glue stick

- Minimize noise and the potential for interruptions.
- You may opt to work on this project in more than one sitting.
- If you experience a notable increase in your stress level while doing this project, take a break.
- As you follow directions, be curious and open to what occurs. Refrain from judging the correctness or quality of your artwork and writing.
- If it's comfortable to do so, close your eyes and consciously enjoy three breaths, being aware of the air moving through your nose or the expansion and contraction of your diaphragm.
- Notice where your body is contacting the chair, floor, or table. Look around the room. Experience a sense of being present in your body and surroundings as you begin.

DIRECTIONS

step 1
Identify 1-3 of your characteristics, qualities, talents, skills, and/or strengths (listed below) that you're grateful to have.

_____

_____

courage	imagination	open-mindedness	hope	honesty	friendliness	practicality	determination
wisdom	resilience	self-acceptance	faith	integrity	enthusiasm	efficiency	willpower
intuition	endurance	self-regulation	grace	fairness	playfulness	competency	forgiveness
curiosity	adaptability	receiving support	humor	kindness	intelligence	productivity	gratitude
learning	willingness	giving support	energy	devotion	optimism	teamwork	mindfulness
creativity	flexibility	problem-solving	love	patience	spirituality	leadership	humility

step 2
No matter what has happened to you or what you have or haven't done in your life, you possess a deep-down quality of basic goodness and worthiness, something in you that is unharmed and essential to your wellbeing and self-worth. Take a moment to get in touch with your basic goodness and worthiness.

Where do you feel this goodness and worthiness in your body? _____

step 3
Look through found and recycled papers (see suggested papers listed in the *PREPARATIONS* section) to find a paper that can represent your basic goodness and worthiness. Describe this paper below.

_____

_____

Why did you pick this specific paper?

_____

step 4
Look through found and recycled papers to find a paper that is imperfect in some way. Describe this paper below. Include a description of the imperfection.

_____

_____

How does this imperfection make this paper more interesting or unique?

_____

_____

What is one of your imperfections that is similar to the imperfection in this paper?

_____

_____

step 5
Look through found and recycled papers to find a paper that doesn't need to impress anyone; it's fine just the way it is. Describe this paper below.

_____

_____

What do you like about this paper?

_____

step 6
Look through found and recycled papers to find a paper showing wear and tear that can represent some of the stress you have experienced in life. Describe this paper below.

_____

Why did you pick this specific paper?

Does this paper have any redeeming qualities? If so, what are they?

step 7
Practice self-compassion.

1. I acknowledge one of my imperfections.
2. I give myself a kind thought and/or gesture, such as taking a conscious breath, patting my head, or hugging myself.
3. I know other people in the world have imperfections similar to mine; I'm not alone.
4. In my mind, I send compassionate thoughts to those people, far and near.

step 8
Look through found and recycled papers to find one that represents renewal. This paper symbolizes the substance needed for careful mending to refurbish a wabi-sabi bowl or cup. It also represents your own self-repair and renewal. Describe this paper below.

Why did you pick this specific paper?

step 9
To construct your wabi-sabi collage, select one of the bowl or cup drawings on the following pages. If you want to use the provided images more than once, trace or photocopy them. Or you may want to draw an asymmetric outline of a bowl of your own design with a chisel-tip black felt pen on a sheet of white mixed media paper.

Tear or cut pieces from the found and recycled papers you chose. As you fit and arrange the papers on the bowl or cup, you may want to use one kind of paper in more than one place. Don't expect your papers to conform perfectly to the outlines of the bowl or to each other. You may want to overlap pieces of paper. Give yourself permission to create an imperfect piece of wabi-sabi art.

Glue the papers onto the bowl design. Cut out your bowl or cup, center it on a white sheet of mixed media paper, and glue it down.

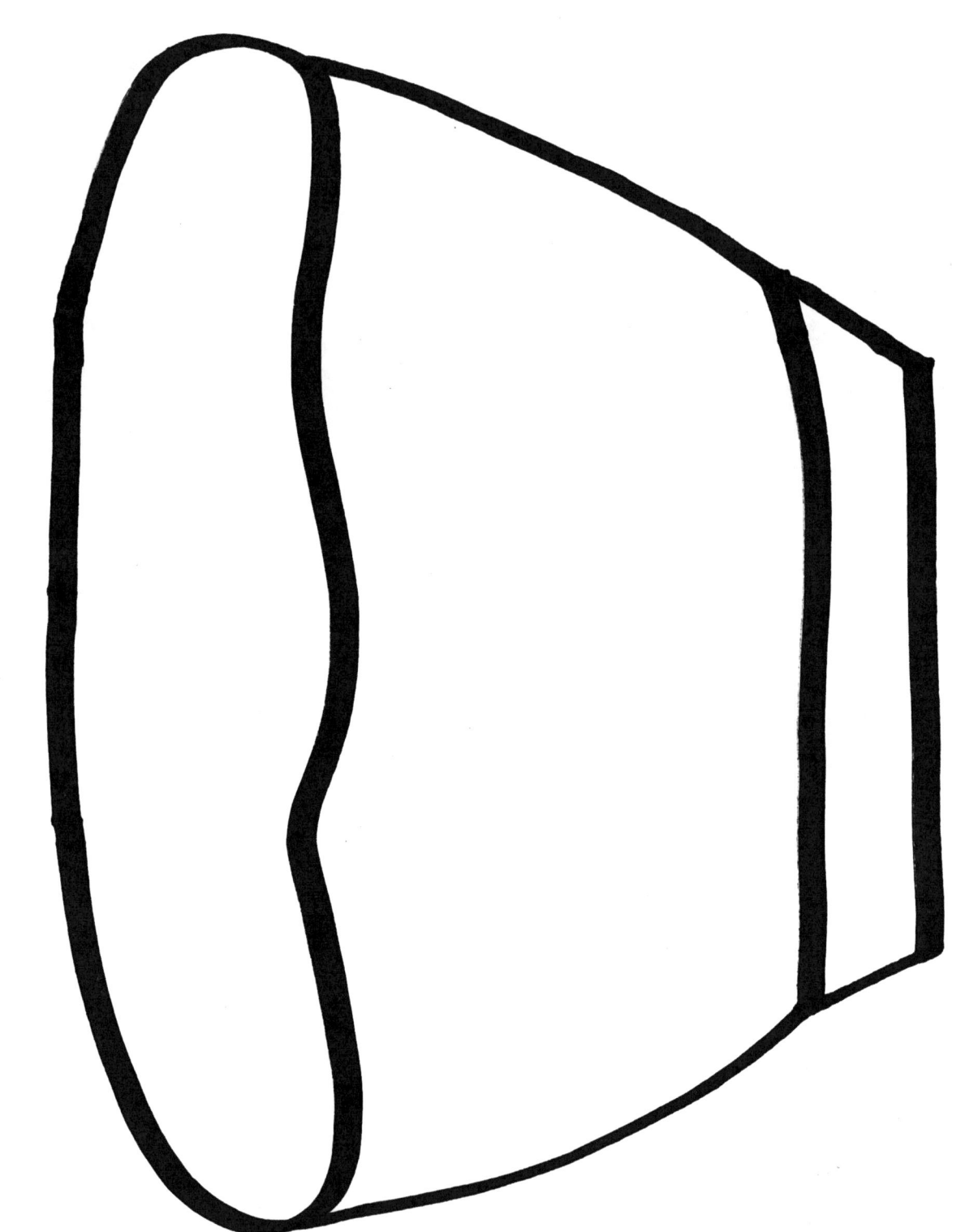

step 10

A Tanka poem is a five-line form of Japanese poetry with no title, no capital letters, no punctuation, and no rhyme.

It's based on a specific form of syllable count for each line:

> line 1: 5 syllables
> line 2: 7 syllables
> line 3: 5 syllables
> line 4: 7 syllables
> line 5: 7 syllables

For each line of your Tanka poem, you'll use words you wrote in different steps of this project, along with any other words you'd like to add.

> line 1: use words you wrote in step 3
> line 2: use words you wrote in step 4
> line 3: use words you wrote in step 5
> line 4: use words you wrote in step 6
> line 5: use words you wrote in step 8

Following are three examples of Tanka poems written by artmakers who have previously completed this project.

> *multi-colored dots*
> *shimmer in the light of day*
> *no need to impress*
> *to smooth scars of life's surface*
> *smell the fresher scent of lime*

> *i am a flower*
> *black sometimes letting doubt in*
> *simple subdued plain*
> *sparkles and shine from dark times*
> *bright pink and yellow waves win*

> *strong uneven spine*
> *in copper-colored goodness*
> *torn but measured space*
> *rounding instead of squaring*
> *as acorns sprout inside me*

Compose your Tanka poem on the blank lines below.

_____

_____

_____

_____

_____

Enjoy reading your poem out loud. Let the rhythm enter your brain and body by allowing the sounds to vibrate through your ears, head, and down to your toes. In this way, you'll enhance your seeing, reading, and hearing experiences.

LIFE APPLICATIONS

- How can you re-envision one of your imperfections as having an element of hidden beauty or being poetic in some way?

- What is something you can let go of if you don't have to try to impress or please others so much?

- What is one way you currently express your authentic self, and another way you would like to express your authentic self in the near future?

- What is something new and fresh you can add to your life for self-repair or renewal?

CONCLUSIONS

- Note any useful insights, revelations, beliefs, or intentions that emerged while you worked on this project or that come to mind now.

- Detect any tension you're holding in your neck, shoulders, or elsewhere in your body. Consciously relax, pat, massage, or gently stretch those areas.
- If it's comfortable to do so, close your eyes and consciously enjoy three breaths.
- Notice where your body is contacting the chair, floor, or table. Look around the room. Experience a sense of being present in your body and surroundings as you finish.
- Sign and date your artwork. Store it for safekeeping.

  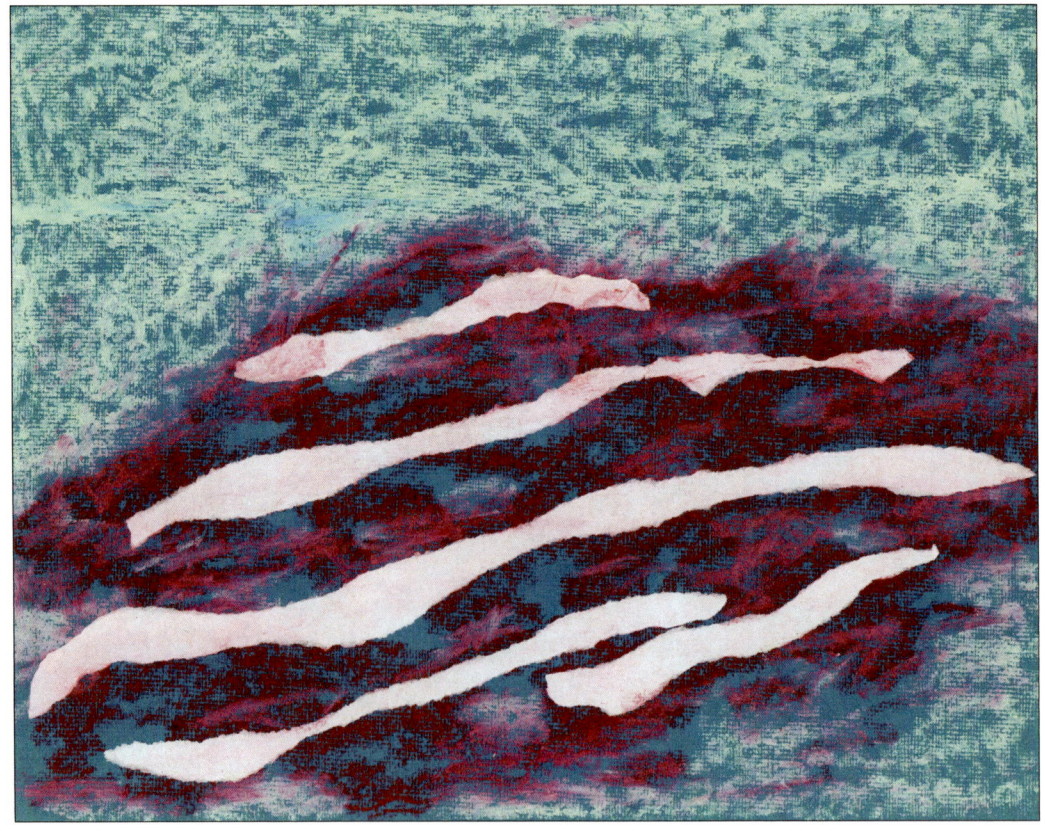

project **9**

RISE ABOVE A RED TIDE OF UNCERTAINTY

choice & action

Uncertainty is caused by our inability to know what the future holds. We cannot precisely predict or control what will happen to us, to our families and friends, or to the world. We may worry whether we'll be able to handle changes as they come our way.

Instead of waiting for the worst to happen (which very well may not occur), we can reduce stress by shifting our focus from wishing we could control the future to making small choices and taking small actions that will influence the quality of our present lives and may also have a positive effect on the future.

Even though we generally tend to think of uncertainty as stressful, it can also open the way for new experiences, positive changes, and living life more fully. Without uncertainty, we would be stuck in monotonous lives and deprived of opportunities to experience a variety of prospects. Staying open to the uncertainty of "not knowing" means that all kinds of things and ways of being might yet be discovered.

In this project you'll work with metaphors of ocean waves and red tides to explore one issue of uncertainty that concerns you now. You'll identify a few strengths, a choice to be made, and a positive possibility to help you rise above the waves of uncertainty with less fear and a little more self-assurance. If you choose to do so, you'll also write a statement of endurance or willpower.

PREPARATIONS

- Clear and protect the surface of your artmaking table.
- Gather tools and materials: pen or pencil for writing
    8½"x11" or 9"x12" assorted solid-color papers
    9"x12" tracing paper, 1 sheet
    oil pastels
    glue stick
    scissors

- Minimize noise and the potential for interruptions.
- You may opt to work on this project in more than one sitting.
- If you experience a notable increase in your stress level while doing this project, take a break.
- As you follow directions, be curious and open to what occurs. Refrain from judging the correctness or quality of your artwork and writing.
- If it's comfortable to do so, close your eyes and consciously enjoy three breaths, being aware of the air moving through your nose or the expansion and contraction of your diaphragm.
- Notice where your body is contacting the chair, floor, or table. Look around the room. Experience a sense of being present in your body and surroundings as you begin.

DIRECTIONS

step 1
What is something in your life that gives you a sense of certainty or control?

_____

_____

step 2
Describe one uncertainty you are experiencing now. This could be related to a future outcome you wish you could have more control over.

_____

_____

_____

_____

step 3

Circle 3-5 words below that relate to this uncertainty.

more trouble	worry	confusion	distrust	negative outcome	indecision	guesswork
uneasiness	anger	urgency	anxiety	worsening conditions	suffering	sadness
misgivings	fear	suspicion	waiting	low confidence	questioning	more work
impatience	doubt	challenge	concern	inability to cope	conflicts	self-doubt
reluctance	hurt	hesitation	threat	disappointment	risk	failure

Where do you feel this uncertainty in your body?

_____

step 4

Choose a solid-color sheet of paper to represent ocean water.

step 5

A red tide is a "bloom" of toxic protozoa that floats near the water's surface close to coastlines. You'll use the metaphor of a red tide to represent the toxicity of stress associated with your uncertainty.

Orient your solid-color paper horizontally or vertically. Choose a red, orange, or brown oil pastel to represent the toxic tide of uncertainty. You can use more than one of these colors if you wish. Imagine you're looking down at the ocean from above. Using the end or side of the oil pastel, add one or more areas of red tide to the surface of the solid-color "ocean" paper.

step 6

Tear 3-5 strips of tracing paper to represent ocean waves. Try tearing from both the long and short sides of the tracing paper to see which effect you like best. You may want to overlap some of the waves. Arrange and glue the waves to your artwork in whatever way makes sense and looks right to you.

step 7

To prevent sinking, drowning, getting caught in the undertow, or having to swim through the toxic tide, circle 1-5 strengths that will help you stay on top of the waves.

courage	imagination	open-mindedness	hope	honesty	friendliness	practicality	determination
wisdom	resilience	self-acceptance	faith	integrity	enthusiasm	efficiency	willpower
intuition	endurance	self-regulation	grace	fairness	playfulness	competency	forgiveness
curiosity	adaptability	receiving support	humor	kindness	intelligence	productivity	gratitude
learning	willingness	giving support	energy	devotion	optimism	teamwork	mindfulness
creativity	flexibility	problem-solving	love	patience	spirituality	leadership	humility

step 8
Read the following statements. Checkmark any that might be helpful to you now, as they apply to the uncertainty you described in step 2.

   By accepting that I cannot be in total control, I experience a sense of relief. It's not all up to me.
   Instead of trying to control this situation by myself, I see myself as a collaborator or team member.
   I can count on my values to guide my choices.
   I have experienced uncertainty many times in the past and made it through.
   This is stressful, but I accept this feeling of uncertainty and practice patience.
   Without uncertainty there would be no possibility for new opportunities or achievements in my life.
   Whatever happens, I can give it my best effort.
   I can make wise choices in the present that will affect my future in a positive way.
   I can live more in the present and spend less time thinking about the future.
   I can get through this time of uncertainty.
   This uncertainty may lead to a positive outcome.
   I can bring joyful effort to this uncertainty, no matter the outcome.
   I commit to carry on, no matter what.

step 9
Related to this uncertainty, can you imagine one positive possibility or outcome that might occur during this period of uncertainty.

_____

step 10
In this step you'll be writing an endurance or willpower statement. Following are two statements from artmakers who have completed this project.

   With determination and enough patience to make my best effort, there is the possibility for a positive outcome to achieve my dream, otherwise I'll bounce back and carry on, greeting a newfound goal. One way or the other, I'll surf the waves until I reach the shore.

   Even if the long-term process is difficult, there will be pleasant times that I can make happen along the way.

Using all or some of the strengths you circled in step 7, one or two statements you checked in step 8, and perhaps the possibility you described in step 9, write an endurance or willpower statement to address the uncertainty you described in step 2.

_____

_____

_____

_____

step 11
Choose an oil pastel color to represent your statement. Add that color to your artwork as an abstract or symbolic shape.

Title your artwork: _____

LIFE APPLICATIONS

- What is one small choice you can make now that might reduce the possibility of a totally negative outcome regarding the uncertainty you described in step 2?

  _____

  When, where, and how can you act on this choice?

  _____

  _____

  Will you need support or advice from others to follow through with your choice and action? If so, who and what kind of support can they provide that will be helpful?

  _____

  _____

  When you've done what you can in the present to influence a better outcome for the future, look to your inner resource of self-trust to realize you'll probably be able to handle the outcome whether it's positive, negative, or something in between. If you need support at that time, trust that you'll be able to find the support you'll need.

- What is one thing you can do today that will give you a sense of accomplishment or a sense of some control?

  _____

- You can repeat this project to address other uncertainties in your life.

CONCLUSIONS

- Note any useful insights, revelations, beliefs, or intentions that emerged while you worked on this project or that come to mind now.

  _____

  _____

- Detect any tension you're holding in your neck, shoulders, or elsewhere in your body. Consciously relax, pat, massage, or gently stretch those areas.
- If it's comfortable to do so, close your eyes and consciously enjoy three breaths.
- Notice where your body is contacting the chair, floor, or table. Look around the room. Experience a sense of being present in your body and surroundings as you finish.
- Sign and date your artwork. Store it for safekeeping.

project 10

SURREALISM FOR THE SAKE OF GOODNESS

curiosity & exploration

One way we can dilute the negative effects of stress is to see and appreciate the beauty and goodness that's right in front of us in our everyday lives. We can savor these positive experiences while they're happening and consciously save them in our memory banks for retrieval during times when our lives are more difficult. These beneficial memories can serve as reminders that we are indeed capable of experiencing goodness in others, the world, and ourselves.

Another way to dilute the impact of stress is to intentionally create good experiences in our lives. These experiences might be linked to recreation, relaxation, hobbies, having fun, or engaging in activities that are interesting, intriguing, or adventurous. We can consciously decide to connect with people we enjoy being with, go to beautiful or inspirational places, and create pleasant sensory experiences.

To be more aware of the goodness in your life, you'll select six small found images of natural or man-made objects that represent recent positive experiences. With these images, you'll assemble a two-dimensional surreal collage. Surrealism juxtaposes unexpected, fanciful, or outlandish imagery to make the unimaginable seem imaginable. Popularized in the early 20th century, surrealism is a movement that remains active today.

If you choose to do so, you can engage in a surreal writing technique called *automatic writing*. You'll complete this project by making a list of ideas to bring more goodness into your life.

PREPARATIONS

- Clear and protect the surface of your artmaking table.
- Gather tools and materials: pencil and eraser
  black ultra-fine pen
  black chisel-tip marker
  scissors
  glue stick
  9"x12" mixed media art paper, 1 sheet
  image sources, such as used magazines, books, newspapers, brochures, catalogs, old calendars, greeting cards, photocopies, online printouts, or your own photos

- Minimize noise and the potential for interruptions.
- You may opt to work on this project in more than one sitting.
- If you experience a notable increase in your stress level while doing this project, take a break.
- As you follow directions, be curious and open to what occurs. Refrain from judging the correctness or quality of your artwork and writing.
- If it's comfortable to do so, close your eyes and consciously enjoy three breaths, being aware of the air moving through your nose or the expansion and contraction of your diaphragm.
- Notice where your body is contacting the chair, floor, or table. Look around the room. Experience a sense of being present in your body and surroundings as you begin.

DIRECTIONS

step 1

Describe a recent event or situation that went reasonably well for you.

_____

_____

_____

How did you contribute to the overall positive effect?

_____

_____

Look through image sources (listed in the above *PREPARATIONS* section) for a small image of a natural or man-made object that captures the essence or feeling of goodness you experienced during or after the positive event or situation.

Loosely trim around the outside edge of the object or cut it into a shape that pleases you.

Describe the object and note the reason you chose it.

_____
_____
_____

step 2

Describe a different situation that left you feeling good about yourself. This situation might relate to something you did recently that reflected your basic goodness, or it might relate to an accomplishment, a skill or talent you used, a positive interaction with another person, a way you took care of yourself, or something else.

_____
_____
_____

Find a small image of a natural or man-made object that captures the essence or feeling of goodness you experienced. Loosely trim around the outside edge of the object or cut it into a shape that pleases you. Describe the object and note the reason you chose it.

_____
_____
_____

step 3

Describe something about the environment of your home, work, or another place that brings a sense of goodness to you.

_____
_____
_____

Find and loosely trim around one small image of a natural or man-made object that symbolizes the essence or feeling of goodness in this environment. Describe the object and note the reason you chose it.

_____
_____
_____

step 4

Identify a person, group, or pet that brings you support, joy, or inspiration. This could be a person you know or someone you have never met who inspires you in a good way.

_____
_____
_____

Find and loosely trim around one image of a natural or man-made object that represents the essence or feeling of goodness that relates to this connection. Describe the object and note the reason you chose it.

_____
_____
_____

step 5

Identify one thing you saw, touched, tasted, smelled, or heard recently that was pleasant, soothing, beautiful, intriguing, healthy, or wonderful.

_____
_____
_____

Find and loosely trim around one small image of a natural or man-made object that represents the essence or feeling of goodness you experienced from this sensory experience. Describe the object and note the reason you chose it.

_____
_____
_____

step 6

Note something about your physical body that is good. It might be that your body allows you to move around in the world or metabolizes the food you eat. Or maybe it's the 100 billion neurons in your brain that aid in thinking and regulating all parts of your body. Perhaps it's your hands and what they're capable of doing and creating.

_____
_____

Find and loosely trim around one small image of a natural or man-made object that represents the essence or feeling of goodness related to your body. Describe the object and note the reason you chose it.

step 7

View the artwork examples at the beginning of this project for a visual reference as you follow the next steps.

Arrange the six images you have chosen on a sheet of mixed media paper so they touch or overlap to create a collage that you can imagine as a surreal sculpture. If needed, draw lines between images to connect them. Experiment with different arrangements before deciding which one you like best.

You may want to leave space at the bottom of the white paper to draw a platform as a base for your sculpture.

When you're satisfied with the arrangement, glue the images to the surface of the white paper. If you have sketched a platform in pencil, you may want to solidify the platform with a pen or marker.

step 8

Hold your artwork at arm's length. Imagine it's a three-dimensional sculpture that stands five to six feet tall and is installed in a gallery or museum space with white floors and walls. Imagine walking around it to view it from different angles. Are any parts of the sculpture in motion?

What sounds or type of music (classical, opera, jazz, folk, rock and roll, reggae, new age, electronic, Latin, rap, world music, country, blues, choir, etc.) would you like to accompany your artwork in the gallery?

step 9

In this step you'll be writing a surrealistic, automatic piece of writing related to your artwork. Following are two examples of writings from artmakers who have previously completed this project.

> *IT'S ABOUT TIME*
>
> *A blue-footed booby flew in from the tropics, wonderlanding a shiny hot pepper to season the blue-ribbon salad of dreams. Push the brass button to ring in the good news about the prize-winning goodness that couldn't wait another minute to be served-up and enjoyed. Sway to the music of electric violins.*

TOOLS OF GOODNESS

A base of artistic tools holds all the weight. Branching off, a magnifying glass for looking closely at life, seeing all the small gifts and signs: the monarch butterfly hatched with help that travels to South America today for the winter, a treasured sand dollar from Higgins Beach that holds the scale, finding balance and grounding, teetering above, a golden mirror that each day reflects back the truth and beauty it sees.

On the following lines, write phrases or sentences that spontaneously come to mind as you look at your surreal sculpture artwork. Allow your writing to flow onto the page before logic has time to take over. Let your uncensored mind do the writing. Simply record thoughts that stream through your consciousness while looking at your artwork. Your writing may be surprising, whimsical, fantastical, or something else altogether.

Write for about 5 minutes. To start your writing, you may want to begin with the phrase: *Goodness is like . . .* or *Notice . . .* Use an additional piece of paper for writing if needed. If you wish, you can title your artwork and writing when finished.

(title)

Read your writing out loud so you can both see and hear it.

LIFE APPLICATIONS

- Before going to sleep at night, remember the good experiences, people, and things in your life that were prominent during the day. If this is helpful, make it a nightly practice.

- On a separate sheet of paper, list 50-100 good things. This list might include your favorite colors, most-liked trees, flowers, or plants; scents and smells you enjoy; healthy food you savor; music you like to listen to; fresh air and water; places you like to visit; kind or supportive people; your favorite interests and activities; things you like to touch; sounds that bring you enjoyment; or your most-liked natural and man-made objects. Read and update it occasionally.

- Consider three small ways to bring more goodness into your life. These might be related to engaging in a new positive activity, validating something unusual about yourself, connecting to others, spending time in a pleasant environment, or practicing your spirituality in a different way. Note how, when, and where you will bring these new experiences of goodness into your life.

    1. _____

    2. _____

    3. _____

- Each day make a conscious effort to bring at least one small experience of goodness into your life and offer one act of kindness to yourself, others, or the world.

CONCLUSIONS

- Note any useful insights, revelations, beliefs, or intentions that emerged while you worked on this project or that come to mind now.

    _____
    _____
    _____

- Detect any tension you're holding in your neck, shoulders, or elsewhere in your body. Consciously relax, pat, massage, or gently stretch those areas.
- If it's comfortable to do so, close your eyes and consciously enjoy three breaths.
- Notice where your body is contacting the chair, floor, or table. Look around the room. Experience a sense of being present in your body and surroundings as you finish.
- Sign and date your artwork. Store it for safekeeping.

project **11**

DEPICT AND RESCRIPT YOUR INNER CRITIC

liberation & transformation

Around age five or six, most of us begin to develop an inner critic. We start to compare ourselves to peers, cultural norms, and ideal media images based on appearances, popularity, capabilities, and possessions. We also begin to internalize criticism that may come from parents, caretakers, other adults, or peers.

Habitual self-criticism is a harmful way of trying to conform to who we think we should be. It can damage our sense of self-trust, self-worth, and confidence. During times of high stress, crisis, or trauma, our inner critics may become increasingly more active, adding to the already adverse effects of stress.

With greater awareness, we can determine when our inner critics are speaking to us in stressful and self-defeating ways. We can hear their voices without buying into their negativity. We can also befriend our inner critics and liberate them by redefining their roles and transforming them from judgmental commentators into compassionate helpers. Instead of being driven by self-criticism, we can be motivated by self-validation and self-support while learning from our mistakes.

Your artwork and writing will help you to better understand your inner critic and move toward establishing a kinder, wiser inner voice. You'll select provided images to construct two figures, one that represents your inner critic and one that represents a transformed version of your inner critic. You'll create a rescripted personal message from your new inner helper.

PREPARATIONS

- Clear and protect the surface of your artmaking table.
- Gather tools and materials: pen or pencil for writing
  scissors
  glue stick
  8½"x11" or 9"x12" assorted solid-color papers

- Minimize noise and the potential for interruptions.
- You may opt to work on this project in more than one sitting.
- If you experience a notable increase in your stress level while doing this project, take a break.
- As you follow directions, be curious and open to what occurs. Refrain from judging the correctness or quality of your artwork and writing.
- If it's comfortable to do so, close your eyes and consciously enjoy three breaths, being aware of the air moving through your nose or the expansion and contraction of your diaphragm.
- Notice where your body is contacting the chair, floor, or table. Look around the room. Experience a sense of being present in your body and surroundings as you begin.

DIRECTIONS

step 1
List 2-5 personal characteristics you're grateful to have. Consider your skills, talents, interests, and any strengths from the list below.

_____

_____

_____

_____

courage	imagination	open-mindedness	hope	honesty	friendliness	practicality	determination
wisdom	resilience	self-acceptance	faith	integrity	enthusiasm	efficiency	willpower
intuition	endurance	self-regulation	grace	fairness	playfulness	competency	forgiveness
curiosity	adaptability	receiving support	humor	kindness	intelligence	productivity	gratitude
learning	willingness	giving support	energy	devotion	optimism	teamwork	mindfulness
creativity	flexibility	problem-solving	love	patience	spirituality	leadership	humility

step 2
Briefly describe a recent situation that activated your inner critic.

What did your inner critic say to you at that time?

How did your inner critic make you feel?

step 3
Circle 1-3 of the following phrases that best describe what it's like when your inner critic is active.

My inner critic . . .

devalues me	makes me think I'm not good enough	makes me think I don't measure up
bullies me	causes me to think it's all my fault	blames or shames me
belittles me	tears me down	is overly hard on me
betrays me	sabotages me	is my own prosecutor and persecutor
nit-picks me	makes me doubt myself	compares me to others
discredits me	thinks I should be perfect	is my own worst enemy
punishes me	calls me a fraud or an imposter	questions my capability

step 4

Cut out the arm, leg, torso, and head shapes on the next page. Photocopy or trace these shapes if you don't want to remove them from the workbook. Set these shapes aside for now.

step 5

View the artwork examples at the beginning of this project for a visual reference as you follow the next artmaking steps.

To construct your inner critic, select 1-3 images from the next four pages. It may be meaningful to use different images to represent different body parts.

Remove the image(s) from the workbook or photocopy them.

Use the body part templates from step 4 to cut out arms, legs, torso, and head from the image(s) you selected. Put a template on top of an image, draw around it, and cut out the body part from the image.

Arrange these parts to form a figure, but *do not* glue them down yet.

Why did you choose the image(s) you selected to represent your inner critic?

_____
_____
_____
_____
_____
_____
_____

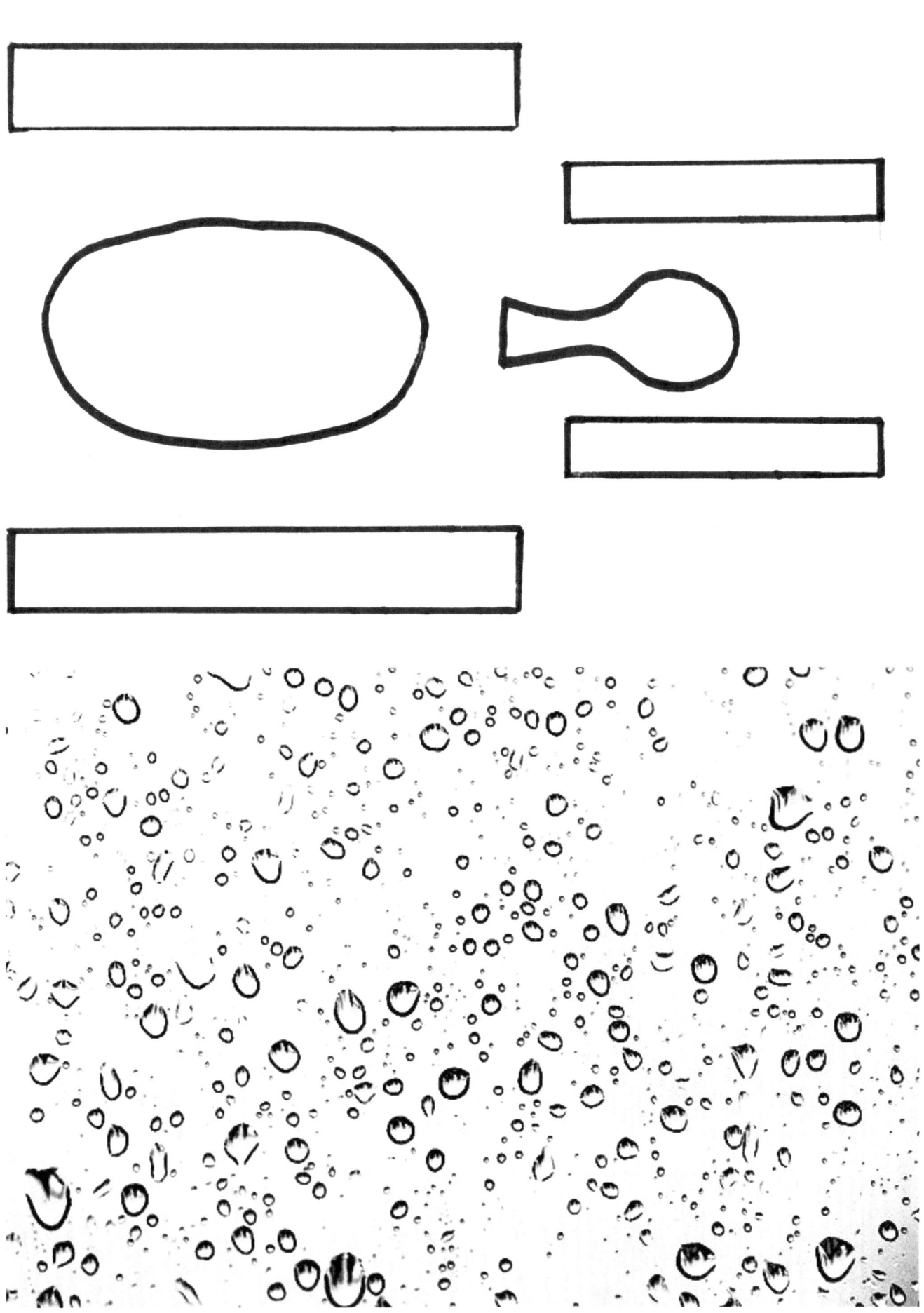

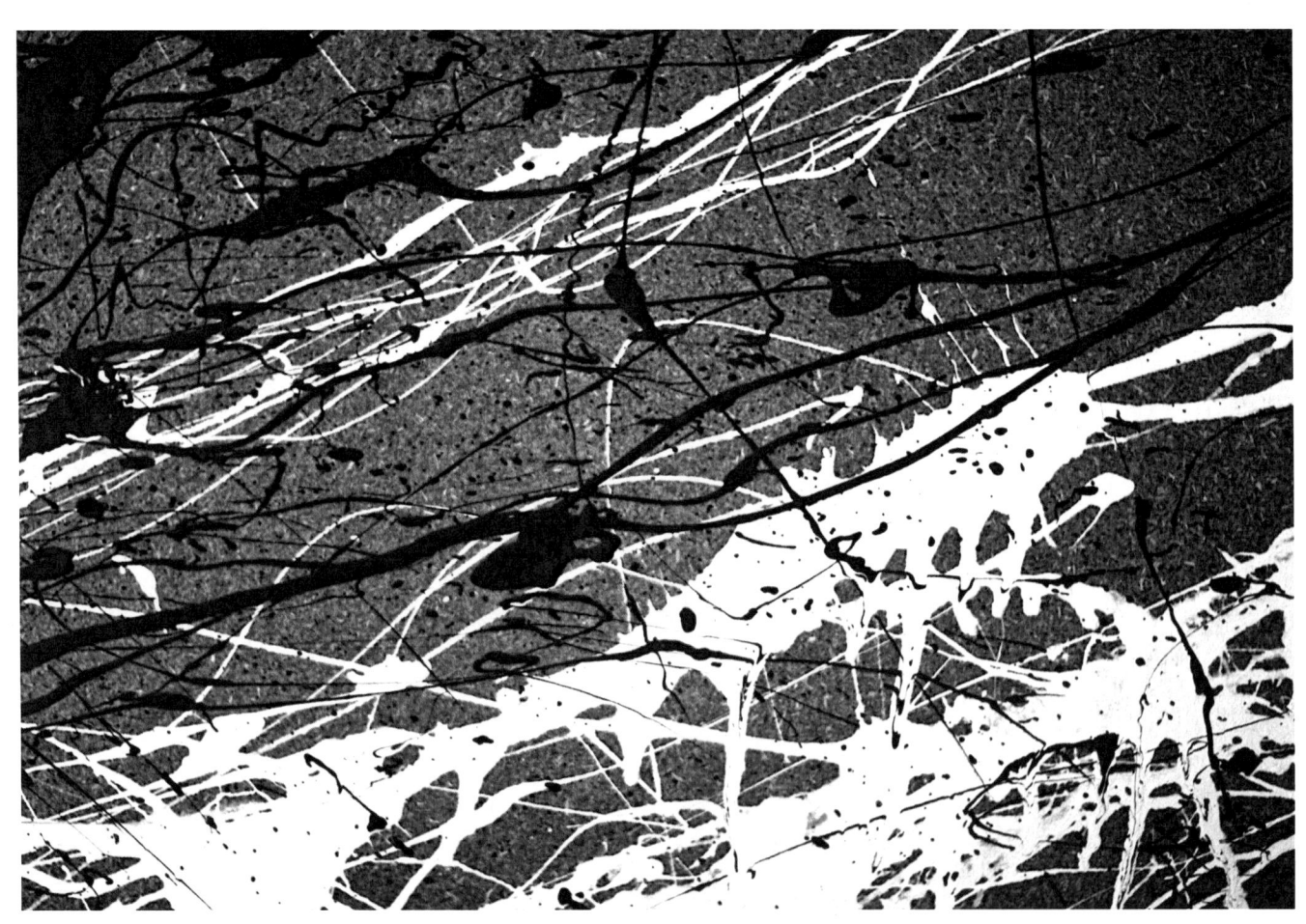

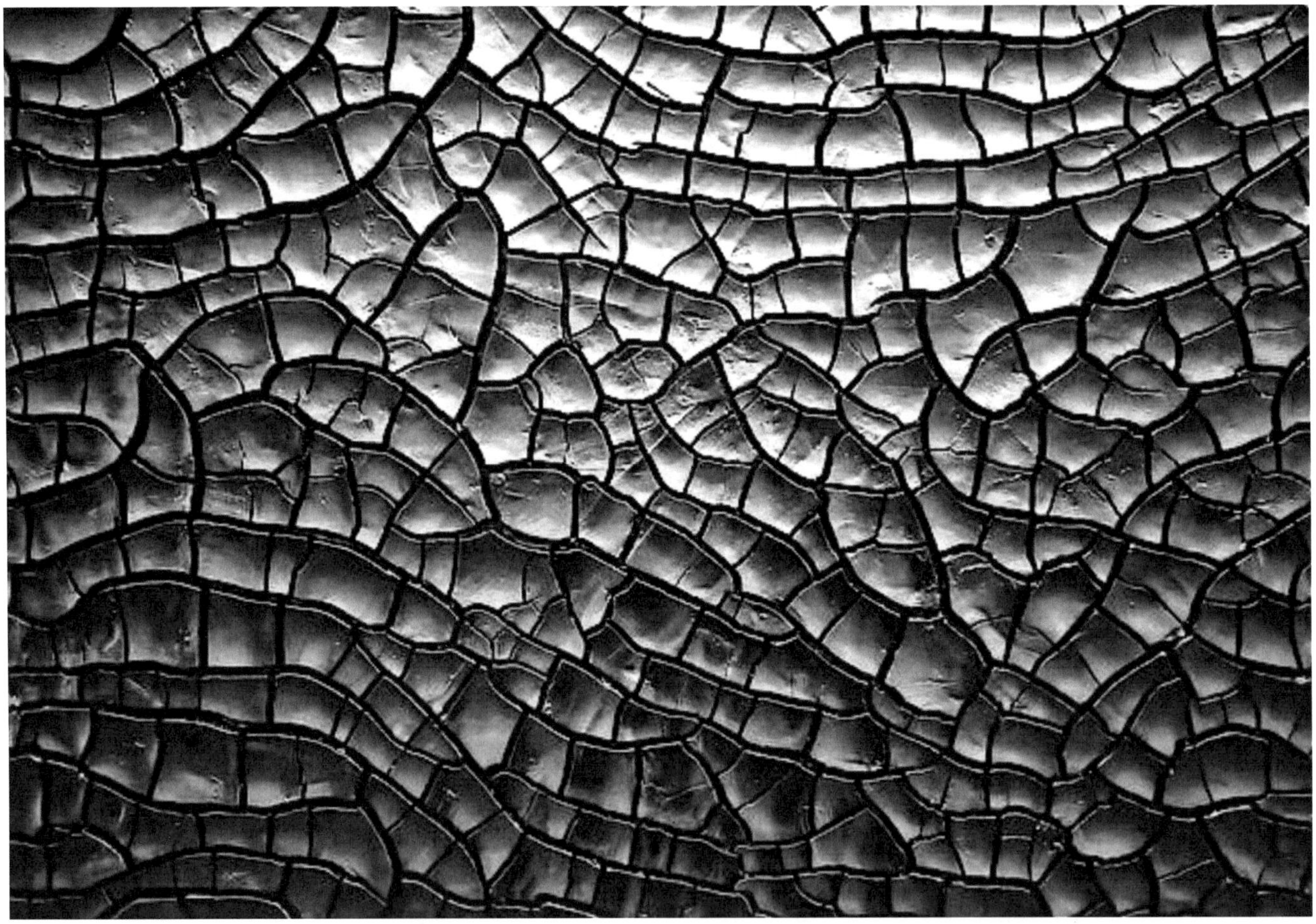

step 6

Look at the inner critic figure you just assembled. Ask your inner critic what it was trying to protect you from or what it was trying to motivate you to do or keep you from doing with its comments in step 2.

Inner critic's answer: _____

_____

Ask your inner critic what it thinks might happen if you don't heed its criticism.

Inner critic's answer: _____

_____

step 7

Let your inner critic know you appreciate its efforts to protect or motivate you, but the way the message was delivered made you doubt yourself and feel stressed. Ask your inner critic if it would be willing to soften the message so its effect can be constructive rather than destructive.

"Instead of being so critical, could you . . . ?"   (Circle 2-5 of the following.)

support me	stand up for me	be my trustworthy confidant
respect me	give me a break	have reasonable expectations
care about me	offer constructive advice	accept my vulnerabilities *and* my strengths
forgive me	advocate for me	show up for me in a good way no matter what
validate me	be more patient	realize I'm trying to do my best
be kind to me	be wise and understanding	help me learn from my mistakes
believe in me	provide goodwill	let me be me

step 8

Read through the four transformative descriptions below. Circle the one that best resonates with how you would like to transform your inner critic.

inner critic → inner helper

inner enemy → inner ally

inner inhibitor → inner promoter

inner judge → inner nurturer

step 9

To construct your transformed inner critic, select 1-3 images from the following four pages. Remove the image(s) from the workbook or photocopy them.

Use the body part templates from step 4 to cut out arms, legs, torso, and head from the image(s) you selected. Put a template on top of an image, draw around it, and cut out the body part from the image.

Arrange these parts to form a figure, but *do not* glue them down yet.

Why did you choose the image(s) you selected to represent your transformed inner critic?

_____
_____
_____
_____
_____
_____
_____
_____
_____
_____

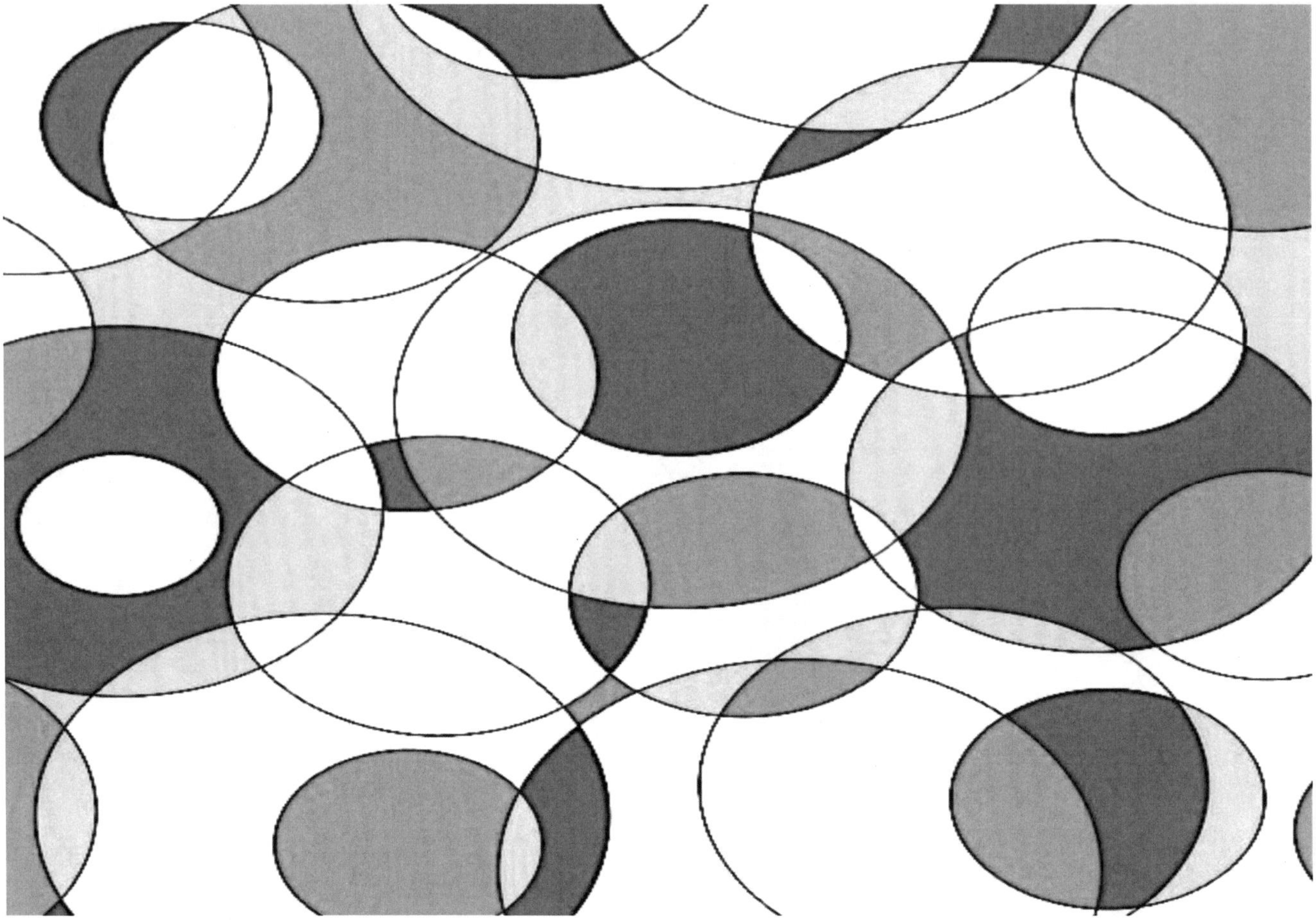

step 10

In this step you'll be writing a message to yourself from your transformed inner critic.

Following are two examples of writing from artmakers who have previously completed this project.

> *Dear Melissa,*
> *You have so many gifts. Please do not hide them or question them. You have tremendous power. Please embrace and use it. Reach for the skies. There is no other you in this world. Your eyes see the world in only the way you can. Your mouth speaks in a way only you can. Your ears hear only the way you can. Your hands create and make in the only way you can. Your mind works only in the way your mind can. You deserve the ground you stand on and the world is better with you in it.*

> *Hey Thomas—you're doing your best job given what you're dealing with. It's not easy to always do the right thing without knowing ahead of time what will happen. You were able to use your courage to speak up for yourself and others. Pat yourself on the back and continue to go forward. You've got what it takes!*

Read what you wrote in step 2 and ask your transformed inner critic to communicate with you in a kinder, more supportive way, giving you constructive positive feedback rather than destructive negative feedback. What helpful feedback can your transformed inner critic offer that might address one or more of the following points and motivate you in a positive way?

- reaching for a goal
- honoring my values in life
- enjoying an activity
- self-understanding
- my best effort

- positive self-characteristics
- being my authentic self
- taking a potentially beneficial risk
- wisdom from making a mistake
- a well-intentioned action

Write a rescripted message to yourself from your inner helper, ally, promoter, or nurturer on the following blank lines.

_____
_____
_____
_____
_____
_____
_____

Read your writing out loud so you can both see and hear it.

step 11
Choose a solid-color sheet of paper to represent self-support.

Assemble and arrange both figures on the paper in a way that has meaning to you. Glue them to the solid-color paper.

What is the significance of the arrangement?

_____
_____
_____
_____

Give your artwork a title. _____

step 12
Ask your inner helper if there is something you could learn from the situation in step 2 or one thing you might think or do differently in a similar situation.

Inner helper's answer: _____

_____
_____
_____
_____
_____

LIFE APPLICATIONS

- Read through the following comparison:

  Destructive self-criticism leads to harsh self-judgment and decreased self-worth. It can activate and promote stress, vulnerabilities, self-doubt, shame, guilt, anxiety, frustration, depression, isolation, and self-impairing behaviors.

  Constructive self-evaluation leads to self-acceptance and increased self-worth. It can activate and promote strengths, values, belief in self, and positive change.

  Which one of the above statements do you prefer to live by?

- Consider keeping a journal to become more aware of when and why your inner critic is activated. Rescript each episode of self-criticism to offer yourself constructive, supportive feedback.

- Remember that making mistakes is part of life. We learn from our mistakes to move forward.

- Practice self-compassion when your inner critic is active.

  1. I acknowledge the self-criticism I'm experiencing.
  2. I give myself a kind thought or gesture, such as crossing my arms over my chest, holding my own hand, or rescripting the message to support myself.
  3. I know other people in the world are experiencing similar self-criticism; I'm not alone.
  4. In my mind, I send compassionate thoughts to those people, far and near.

- Each day, let your transformed inner helper validate or motivate you. What is something your inner helper can say to validate or motivate you today?

  _____

  _____

- You can revisit your art and writing from this project if their messages and insights can benefit you in your ongoing efforts and successes to befriend yourself.

CONCLUSIONS

- Note any useful insights, revelations, beliefs, or intentions that emerged while you worked on this project or that come to mind now.

  _____

  _____

- Detect any tension you're holding in your neck, shoulders, or elsewhere in your body. Consciously relax, pat, massage, or gently stretch those areas.
- If it's comfortable to do so, close your eyes and consciously enjoy three breaths.
- Notice where your body is contacting the chair, floor, or table. Look around the room. Experience a sense of being present in your body and surroundings as you finish.
- Sign and date your artwork. Store it for safekeeping.

project **12**

UNFOLD A CRISIS-PROPELLED PLAN

options & outcomes

NOTE: This project is designed for people who are currently experiencing a crisis. If you're in crisis and your stress becomes unmanageable or you might benefit from seeking professional help, contact a knowledgeable counselor, find an appropriate support group, or call a local or national mental health hotline. Most people in crisis need support of one kind or another if only from friends or family.

Across each of our lifetimes, it's inevitable that we'll experience at least a handful of crises. Typically, a crisis begins with a highly stressful event or sudden change in circumstances, accompanied by a disruption in normal routines or a threat to important goals. It may involve one person, a family, or a community, and will typically last four to six weeks or longer. New skills and outside supports may be needed to deal with a crisis.

During a crisis, our sense of mental and emotional space closes in and our physical bodies frequently tighten up. We may experience denial and confusion along with a sense of urgency. Without all the facts, we may rush into making decisions and taking actions that can make the situation worse. If possible, we need to give ourselves time to consider what has happened, what is still happening, and what might happen in the near future, so we can make better choices about what to do or what not to do to alleviate stress instead of compounding it.

The overall goals of crisis management are to improve safety and day-to-day functioning, while dealing with critical problems. A crisis may eventually culminate with a positive result, a negative outcome, or a mixed conclusion. It's not always possible to return to what was previously normal before a crisis, but with time and effort, progress can prevail, and life may turn out to be as good or even better than before.

You'll choose a solid-color sheet of paper to represent your crisis and fold it inward to symbolize the need for protection. To lessen the potential for being overwhelmed, you'll identify separate tasks instead of taking on the whole crisis all at once. You'll also identify helpful strengths and supports and distinguish between stress-driven reactions and adaptive responses to the crisis at hand.

PREPARATIONS

- Clear and protect the surface of your artmaking table.
- Gather tools and materials: pen or pencil for writing
  ruler
  8½"x11" or 9"x12" assorted solid-color papers
  9"x12" white mixed media paper, cut into twelve 2"x 2" squares
  scissors
  glue stick
  image sources, such as used magazines, books, newspapers, brochures, catalogs, old calendars, greeting cards, photocopies, online printouts, or your own photos

- Minimize noise and the potential for interruptions.
- You may opt to work on this project in more than one sitting.
- If you experience a notable increase in your stress level while doing this project, take a break.
- As you follow directions, be curious and open to what occurs. Refrain from judging the correctness or quality of your artwork and writing.
- If it's comfortable to do so, close your eyes and consciously enjoy three breaths, being aware of the air moving through your nose or the expansion and contraction of your diaphragm.
- Notice where your body is contacting the chair, floor, or table. Look around the room. Experience a sense of being present in your body and surroundings as you begin.

DIRECTIONS

step 1
Look through image sources (listed above in the *PREPARATIONS* section) for a small abstract, semi-abstract, or realistic image that is soothing to you and offers kindness and compassion. This image may contain colors, shapes, lines, people, animals, indoor or outdoor scenes, natural or man-made objects, art reproductions, or other visual elements. If you prefer, you can create your own small abstract or semi-symbolic image that provides comfort and soothing.

Place the image on the tabletop where you can look at it from time to time while you work on this project. What meaning does this image hold for you?

---

step 2
Briefly describe the crisis you're currently experiencing.

Describe facts (not opinions) which led to the crisis: what, when, where, who.

We often hold or shorten our breath from time to time during a crisis. Take a deep breath and exhale slowly. Take another deep breath and sigh as you exhale.

step 3
Circle 1-3 of the following words that best describes the crisis:

catastrophe	overload	peril	predicament	calamity	debacle	setback
emergency	fiasco	chaos	trial by fire	upheaval	bad break	disaster
tribulation	ordeal	defeat	freak-out	blunder	impasse	urgency
entanglement	plight	pressure	misfortune	tragedy	accident	trouble
pandemonium	havoc	loss	devastation	turmoil	desperation	alarm

step 4
As far as the crisis is concerned, what is happening now?

_____

_____

step 5
Circle 1-5 words that describe your current emotional and mental state-of-being as it relates to the crisis.

miserable	fearful	shocked	lonely	numb
rageful	jealous	impulsive	regretful	resentful
infuriated	guilty	panicked	disappointed	confused
aggravated	threatened	impatient	grieved	insecure
rebellious	suspicious	anxious	heartbroken	despairing
dreading	envious	agitated	gloomy	disgraced
irritated	repulsed	chaotic	apprehensive	humiliated
frustrated	angry	embarrassed	uneasy	muddled
conflicted	mistrustful	overwhelmed	defensive	cautious

step 6
Has this crisis affected you physically? If so, how?

_____

Has this crisis affected you in other ways? If so, how?

_____

_____

Has this crisis affected other people? If so, who and how?

_____

_____

Acknowledging the seriousness of the crisis is important. To begin to build resilience and perspective, you may want to consider whether this crisis could have been worse, even though it's critical.

step 7

Why is it important for you to deal with this crisis instead of avoiding it?

___

___

___

What do you need to accept about this situation that you may be overlooking or denying?

___

___

___

If helpful, take one or more deep breaths and consciously relax your muscles.

step 8

View the art and writing photograph at the beginning of this project as you follow the instructions below.

Select a sheet of solid-color paper to represent the crisis.

Fold one corner of the paper in toward the center of the sheet. Keep it folded.

Turn the direction of the paper to fold in another corner of the paper toward the center. This fold may or may not overlap part of the first fold. Keep both folds folded.

Turn the direction of the paper again to fold a third corner toward the center. This fold may also overlap previous folds. Keep it folded along with the other folds.

Turn the direction of the paper once more and fold the fourth corner toward the center.

If there are any edges of the sheet of paper that aren't yet folded inward, fold them toward the center. Tighten the folds by going over them with the edge of a scissors handle.

Open the sheet of paper. Notice how the fold lines go in several directions. Crisis management typically doesn't go forward in a perfectly straight line but proceeds in multiple directions.

step 9

Select a sheet of solid-color paper to represent self-compassion and comforting.

Fold the crisis-colored sheet of paper back up. Place it on top of this compassion-colored paper. Draw around the outer edge of the folded paper shape to create a shape on the compassion-colored paper.

Cut this shape out by cutting inside the outline by about an eighth of an inch.

Fit this cut out shape into the centermost area of the folded paper.

If needed, trim the small image you chose in step 1 so it will fit on the compassion-colored shape. Glue it to the solid-color compassion shape.

Receive the comfort and kindness this image offers you.

Open your artwork. Notice how the folded lines lead your eye inward as well as outward. Crisis management typically requires both inner and outer resources.

step 10

During a crisis we often neglect our physical self-care when it's most needed. It's important to attend to healthy nutrition and hydration. Exercise can aid in tension release. Adequate sleep and rest help you to improve thinking for better decision-making. Excessive alcohol or drug use will make a crisis worse.

What is one small pledge to yourself that will promote your physical self-care during this time of crisis? Write this pledge on a 2"x 2" piece of white paper. Place this inside your folded paper under the mounted image for safekeeping.

step 11

Circle 3-5 strengths you need as you deal with the crisis now.

courage	imagination	open-mindedness	hope	honesty	friendliness	practicality	determination
wisdom	resilience	self-acceptance	faith	integrity	enthusiasm	efficiency	willpower
intuition	endurance	self-regulation	grace	fairness	playfulness	competency	forgiveness
curiosity	adaptability	receiving support	humor	kindness	intelligence	productivity	gratitude
learning	willingness	giving support	energy	devotion	optimism	teamwork	mindfulness
creativity	flexibility	problem-solving	love	patience	spirituality	leadership	humility

How, when, and where will you specifically use one of these strengths?

_____

_____

_____

Write each strength you circled on a 2"x 2" piece of white paper. Place these inside the folded paper under the mounted image for safekeeping.

step 12

What supportive individuals, groups, and organizations can you contact that might be helpful? Do you need the help of any professionals (doctors, counselors, lawyers, etc.)?

Write each of these sources of support on a 2"x 2" piece of white paper. Place them inside the folded paper under the mounted image for safekeeping.

step 13

List any vital life tasks and responsibilities you need to continue to do during this crisis.

_____
_____
_____
_____

To conserve your energy, which daily tasks can you eliminate or postpone for the time being?

_____
_____

Are there any responsibilities or daily tasks you can delegate to others? Who can you count on?

_____
_____

step 14

When a crisis first strikes, people often question whether they'll be able to deal with it. Instead of asking yourself *if* you'll be able to handle this crisis, ask yourself *how* you'll be able to handle it.

Even though a crisis usually involves a complex number of issues, it can be helpful to approach a crisis by breaking it down into smaller components instead of being overwhelmed by the crisis as-a-whole.

Identify the most crucial issue or problem that needs attention right away.

_____
_____

Can this issue or problem be broken down into smaller components? If so, what is the first component you need to deal with?

_____

List 2-3 options to deal with this first component.

_____

_____

_____

Ask yourself if each of the options above is driven by detrimental, stress reactions or by beneficial, adaptive responses. Circle the option that seems to be the best current choice.

If you need help with deciding which option is best, who will you contact? _____

Once an option is chosen, when and how will you act on this choice?

_____

_____

step 15

On a separate sheet of paper, create a to-do list of issues and problems you may need to deal with in the next few days or weeks. Even though this list may change as you move forward, it will help you organize your strategy and clear your mind to some degree. If you like, fold this list up and place it inside your artwork. Keep it handy to monitor your progress and update it when needed.

step 16

In this step you'll be writing a note of encouragement to yourself. Following are two examples of writing from artmakers who have previously completed this project.

> *Even though I'm both overwhelmed and dazed now, if I go step-by-step and day-by-day, I'll do what I need to do. I've gotten through hardships before, and I'll do it again. My practicality, kindness, and wisdom will help me to endure. I can get advice from people at the hospital and my friends will chip in when I ask them. I'll keep up with meditation and healthy eating. I'll let go of unnecessary suffering while practicing compassion for those involved and for myself. I can look up at the sky and welcome the sun each day.*

> *First off, I can take a deep breath before I make any hard decisions. I need to gather my willpower and lean on my ability to adapt. Resilience will be my best friend. I can stay open to knowing this will pass. One way or the other I'll take care of what is most important - the children, the dog, and the bills. I'll make sure I eat and sleep the best I can. I'll get support from my grandmother and reach out to a support group as soon as I find the right fit.*

Write your encouragement note below. You may want to include some of the following phrases in your writing:

I can do this.	My _____ (list strengths circled in step 11) will carry me through.
I can ask for help.	I take care of myself so I can take care of others.
one decision at a time	I practice self-compassion every day.
rest and relax	This level of _____ (words circled in step 5) won't last forever.
slow and sure	Step-by-step I will get through this.
be brave	Given the circumstances, I'm doing the best I can do.
I can feel my feelings.	I'm asking for and accepting support.
breathe deeply	I stay open to possible options and solutions.
I can be safe.	I can give myself the time I need to heal.

_____

_____

_____

_____

_____

_____

_____

_____

_____

_____

_____

_____

_____

_____

Read your writing out loud so you can both see and hear it.

Rewrite this note on a separate sheet of paper. Place it inside the folded paper.

If you can, read this note to yourself every day until the crisis has passed. Write a new note of encouragement if and when you need to.

LIFE APPLICATIONS

- If possible, move forward each day in some small way. Follow the process below if it's helpful. Remember, self-care comes first. Be sure to factor-in some time for self-care, no matter how little time you have to spare.

    1. Identify one problematic issue or concern that needs your attention now.
    2. Can this issue or concern be broken down into smaller, more manageable units?
    3. List alternative choices for action.
    4. Choose the best stress-reducing and most beneficial alternative.
    5. Make a step-by-step plan to act on the best alternative.
    6. Implement the first step.
    7. Evaluate your progress. Revise your plan when needed.

- How will you know when the worst of this crisis is over?

_____

How will your state-of-being change?

increasing relief	less intense emotions	more optimistic	liberated
more secure	able to function better	improved relationships	calmer
less worried	more engaged in life	accept new normal	more at ease

other: _____

- If your life has been permanently altered by the crisis, what is one way you can begin to create a new life that will be a step in the right direction for you?

_____

- Many crises involve loss of one kind or another. Allow yourself time to grieve associated losses.

- You may want to write additional encouraging notes to yourself as time moves forward. You can acknowledge progress you've made and write new to-do lists. Include these inside your artwork.

CONCLUSIONS

- Note any useful insights, revelations, beliefs, or intentions that emerged while you worked on this project or that come to mind now.

_____

_____

- Detect any tension you're holding in your neck, shoulders, or elsewhere in your body. Consciously relax, pat, massage, or gently stretch those areas.
- If it's comfortable to do so, close your eyes and consciously enjoy three breaths.
- Notice where your body is contacting the chair, floor, or table. Look around the room. Experience a sense of being present in your body and surroundings as you finish.
- Sign and date your artwork. Store it for safekeeping.

project 13

ENLIVEN THE TEXTURE OF YOUR LIFE

enhancement & change

Two primary goals of mental health and wellness therapies are to improve day-to-day level of functioning and increase positive life experiences. To work toward these goals, it's helpful to be aware of how we live our lives now and how we'd prefer to live them in the near future.

Without this awareness, we may get caught up in everyday stress, dreariness, or drudgery of daily tasks. We may become exhausted or depressed and wake up in the morning with little motivation or a sense of dread or desperation. It may be hard to imagine that our lives can be any different than they are now.

If we begin by clearing away just one small negative stress factor, we may experience a small opening for improvement. In this way we gradually start to reclaim and transform our lives.

Our optimal sense of aliveness exists when our awareness is focused on the present moment. We can learn to practice the art of mindful living, continuously being open to experiencing and creating our unfolding aliveness as it's happening.

You'll be collecting textured items from around your environment to make oil pastel rubbings for a collage. You'll also follow provided directions to compose an acrostic poem, in which consecutive lines of a poem begin with alphabet letters that vertically spell out a word. In this case, the word you spell will be *ALIVE*.

PREPARATIONS

- Clear and protect the surface of your artmaking table.
- Gather tools and materials: pen or pencil for writing
    9"x12" tracing paper, 1 sheet
    9"x12" mixed media paper, 1 sheet (optional)
    scissors
    glue stick
    8½"x11" or 9"x12" assorted solid-color papers
    white scrap paper
    oil pastels
    paper towel
    3-5 highly textured items such as a cheese grater, mesh strainer, colander, slotted spatula, comb, netting, basket, metal or plastic grids, etc.
- Minimize noise and the potential for interruptions.
- You may opt to complete this project in more than one sitting.
- If you experience a notable increase in your stress level while doing this project, take a break.
- As you follow directions, be curious and open to what occurs. Refrain from judging the correctness or quality of your artwork and writing.
- If it's comfortable to do so, close your eyes and consciously enjoy three breaths, being aware of the air moving through your nose or the expansion and contraction of your diaphragm.
- Notice where your body is contacting the chair, floor, or table. Look around the room. Experience a sense of being present in your body and surroundings as you begin.

DIRECTIONS

step 1

What is something in the past or present that gives you a sense of being truly alive? This could be a specific place, activity, relationship, or situation.

_____

_____

_____

Circle 2-3 words below that describe your above state of aliveness.

calm	refreshed	zestful	satisfied	purposeful	contented	inspired
dynamic	happy	motivated	energetic	directed	empowered	upbeat
creative	animated	invigorated	enlivened	encouraged	enthusiastic	pleased
vitalized	elated	exuberant	awake	spirited	at ease	hopeful
passionate	joyful	emboldened	playful	exhilarated	delighted	merry
lucid	liberated	gleeful	radiant	engaged	luminous	vibrant

Select a solid-color sheet of paper to represent the words you circled above or to represent being awake, alert, and truly alive. Set this sheet of paper aside for later use.

step 2

Be aware that your state of aliveness may vary depending on circumstances, season of the year, time of day, and even the weather. Circle 2-3 words that describe how you feel when you're less alive in your life.

overwhelmed	murky	gloomy	obscured	listless	unappealing
desolate	overcast	bored	dark	numb	overshadowed
dull	foggy	dread	dismal	apathetic	empty
bland	lethargic	lonely	unpleasant	spiritless	lifeless
undesirable	sad	depressed	discouraged	dim	tired
low energy	weary	hopeless	drowsy	sluggish	drab
withdrawn	restless	detached	stressed-out	burned-out	flat

Select a solid-color sheet of paper to represent these words. Set this sheet of paper aside for later use.

step 3

To experiment with creating oil pastel rubbings, place white scrap paper over one of the highly textured surfaces you have collected.

With the end and side of an oil pastel, rub over the surface of the paper. See what effect you get with light pressure compared to heavy pressure.

Continue to experiment by rubbing an oil pastel over scrap paper placed on top of each textured surface.

step 4

Cut a sheet of tracing paper in half. Put it on top of one of the textured surfaces. Select an oil pastel color to represent the feeling of aliveness. Rub the oil pastel over the tracing paper.

Put the same piece of tracing paper on top of a different textured surface. Select a second color to represent aliveness. Rub this color over the tracing paper.

Select a third textured surface and a third color to represent aliveness. Place the same previously colored tracing paper on top of the third textured surface. Rub the third color on top of the previous colors.

step 5

Place the tracing paper rubbing on top of the solid-color sheet of paper you selected in step 1. Then place it on top of the other solid-color sheet of paper you selected in step 2. Notice the different effects of the two solid-color backgrounds on the appearance of the tracing paper rubbing.

step 6

Create a collage with your tracing paper rubbing and the two solid-color sheets of paper. You may want to use one or both solid-color sheets as a background for your collage. You can tear or cut the solid-color sheets and tracing paper rubbing as you wish. Glue your collage components to one of the solid-color sheets or a piece of white mixed media paper. Glue the rubbing face down if you want to avoid smearing.

step 7

Turn your artwork upside down and sideways. Which direction do you prefer? Title your artwork.

step 8

Look at your artwork. Imagine that the different components can move. Circle any words that describe their different movements or lack of motion if that is the case.

MOTIONLESS: inert immobile stagnant stuck dug in

SLOW: crawl creep amble dawdle lope stagger shuffle flounder slink trudge traipse slither waddle waver limp stroll float drift tiptoe sway wobble roam rove wander falter glide

MEDIUM SPEED: hop prance promenade sashay sail scamper scramble scoot march skip slide soar strut canter trot jump jerk rock jaunt sprint spurt twirl flow jitter swoop flail stride bob-up bob-down walk swim skid lurch

FAST: chase dart dash dive gallop hurl hurry propel race run rush scurry speed spin spring sprint skitter streak swerve swing snap whisk zip zoom zap plummet thrash plunge shove smash stomp swat surge gush crash leap lunge slam nab pounce snatch trounce

VARIOUS SPEEDS: careen pivot swivel oscillate undulate vibrate quiver twitch fluctuate roll kick vacillate teeter-totter wiggle bounce writhe twist fly sweep climb fall flap reel pour tremble shiver blow bump collide jab jerk scrawl skim tumble drive dance

step 9

Imagine your artwork can make sounds. Circle 2-3 of the following words that describe those sounds.

SILENCE: quiet hush lull

LOW LEVEL SOUNDS: sigh drip click hum gurgle squeak tap whir tinkle murmur shush slosh swish squish wheeze whish whoosh ping rustle mutter chirrup chirp fizz sizzle flutter slurp snap purr peep rumble whisper tick-tock

MEDIUM LEVEL SOUNDS: ring buzz chatter clank clack crackle echo jingle jangle chime splash thrum thump clatter clip-clop crunch yap rat-a-tat sizzle splat thud squawk beep clap cluck bleat bray cackle hoot snort trill hiss whistle slurp laugh singing

LOUD SOUNDS: bang boom clang rattle roar screech boom pop varoom bellow blare blast bark honk scream thunder shout howl shriek honk

step 10

Although it may not be possible to continually sustain a greater degree of aliveness in your life, even a small boost from time to time can provide significant benefits.

When you're experiencing an improved sense of aliveness, imagine whether you would be living your life more in the present instead of focusing on the past or future. Would you feel all or only some of your emotions? Would connections with others, yourself, and the world be better? Would you be more open and flexible? Imagine and describe how your life might be different with a slight improvement in your sense of aliveness.

_____

_____

_____

_____

_____

_____

_____

_____

step 11

In this step you'll begin writing an acrostic poem in which each line starts with a letter spelling out the word, *ALIVE*. Following are two examples of acrostic poems written by artmakers who have completed this project.

ALIVE

*A*cknowledge the dismal, the murky, the gloom.
*L*earn to seek the fluttering joy, singing play, whistling awake.
*I*nvite light and color to the darkness.
*V*ent the thunder, lightning, storms.
*E*merge each moment, each day.

ALIVE

*A*dequate is not good enough.
*L*aughter is being in the moment.
I sprout a rat-a-tat-tat when setting forth.
*V*enturous visions hum and sing in my head.
*E*nergy is anywhere and everywhere.

Write your acrostic poem below. You'll use the consecutive letters, A, L, I, V, E, as the first letter of a word to begin each line of a five-line poem. Look back through this project to spark your creativity. You may find printed, circled, or written words in the project that start with the letters, A, L, I, V, E. You can also use words from the following list or other words that come to mind. You may want to incorporate words you circled in steps 1-2 and 7-8.

A: activate   abide   accelerate   access   accept   accrue   adapt   adopt   add   advance   affirm   after   aglow   alert   awake   amend   amplify   amid   amuse   animate   appeal

L: launch   laughing   lavish   leap   learn   listen   levity   liberate   life   lift   light   lighten   live   lively   look   loud and clear   love   loving   lucid   lucky   luminous   lark

I: identify   if   I   illuminate   illumination   illustrious   imagine   imbue   impel   incentive   improve   improvise   inasmuch as   increase   indicate   induce   influence   inform   infuse

V: venture   validate   value   variety   vast   velvety   verbalize   verify   versed   via   victory   view   vim   visible   vision   visit   vibrant   vital   vivid   vivify   voice   voluminous   vow

E: energize   eager   ease   enlighten   elevate   effervescent   elated   elicit   elixir   emphasize   embody   encompass   endure   enchanted   engage   enrapture   enthusiasm   exuberance

Write your poem on the blank lines below.

A _____

L _____

I _____

V _____

E _____

Read your poem out loud so you can both see and hear it.

LIFE APPLICATIONS

- Being more alive in your life is linked to physical self-care. Paying attention to basics can influence your overall sense of being healthier and happier.

    What is one small improvement related to nutrition, hydration, exercise, sleep, physical or dental exams, or follow-up recommendations you can realistically commit to?

    _____

- Identify a small negative factor in your life that stifles your energy. How can you limit or eliminate this factor so you can open the potential for increased vitality?

    _____
    _____

- Identify one specific thing you can expand on or add to your life that will increase your sense of aliveness.

    _____

    When, where, and how will you increase this or add it to your life? Be specific.

    _____
    _____

- You can revisit your art and writing from this project if their messages and insights can help to improve your sense of aliveness. Repeat this project if and when it would be beneficial for you.

CONCLUSIONS

- Note any useful insights, revelations, beliefs, or intentions that emerged while you worked on this project or that come to mind now.

    _____
    _____

- Detect any tension you're holding in your neck, shoulders, or elsewhere in your body. Consciously relax, pat, massage, or gently stretch those areas.
- If it's comfortable to do so, close your eyes and consciously enjoy three breaths.
- Notice where your body is contacting the chair, floor, or table. Look around the room. Experience a sense of being present in your body and surroundings as you finish.
- Sign and date your artwork. Store it for safekeeping.

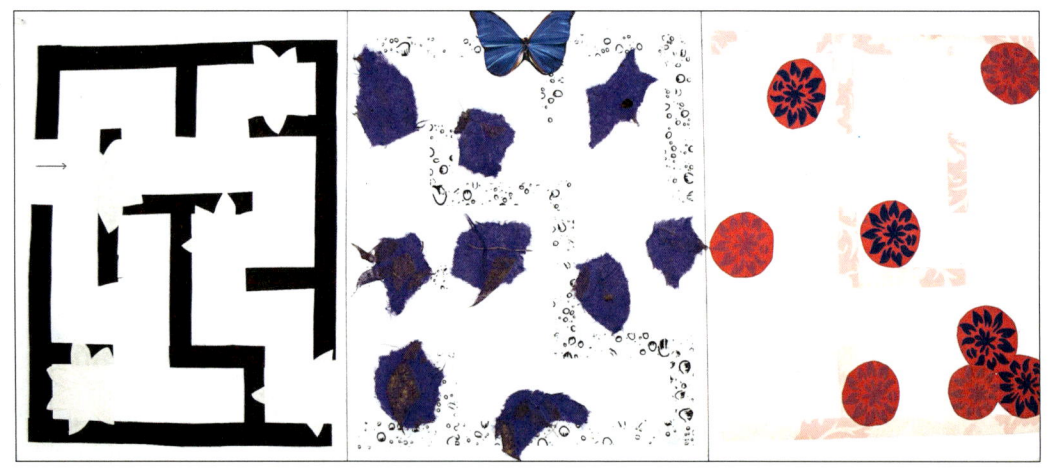

project 14

IN AND OUT OF A MAZE
trauma & aftereffects

NOTE: This project is designed for people who have witnessed or experienced traumatic events or situations that have involved actual or threatened bodily injury or death. This severe form of stress is associated with life-threatening medical emergencies, illnesses, and surgeries; physical abuse or neglect; serious natural and man-made disasters; domestic and sexual violence, assaults, war exposure, and other violent acts. It's best if you can share the details of your trauma story in a safe and supportive environment with a knowledgeable counselor or therapist.

Following severe stress linked to trauma, most people experience negative aftereffects that may last weeks, months, or years. Examples of aftereffects include—but aren't limited to—anxiety, depression, hopelessness, exhaustion, insomnia, numbness, confusion, decreased sense of safety, helplessness, trauma-related nightmares and flashbacks, and significant changes in self-image. Aftereffects may keep people stuck in the past, preventing them from living fully in the present. For some people, the aftereffects may be worse than the initial traumatic event or situation.

It can be helpful to compassionately acknowledge an extremely difficult time in your life with the goal of accepting, reducing, or releasing the aftereffects. Even though you cannot change what happened to you in the past, you may be able to lessen the impact it has on the quality of your life in the present and future.

Using a maze design and found papers, you'll construct a bird's eye view of a maze. Much like trauma and its aftereffects, a maze is a complicated network of paths that can be perplexing, frustrating, and overwhelming. Bewildering routes, obstacles, and mistaken shortcuts add to the many challenges of moving through a maze.

In this project, you'll acknowledge a traumatic event or situation and the aftereffects you've experienced. With writing, you'll imagine what it might be like in the future as you continue your recovery to reach a more open space where the negative aftereffects may not be as intense or frequent.

PREPARATIONS

- Clear and protect the surface of your artmaking table.
- Gather tools and materials: pen or pencil for writing
  - black ultra-fine pen
  - scissors
  - glue stick
  - 9"x12" white mixed media paper, 3 sheets
  - assorted solid-color papers
  - tape
  - image sources, such as used magazines, books, newspapers, brochures, catalogs, old calendars, greeting cards, photocopies, online printouts, or your own photos
  - found or recycled papers, such as used bags, maps, envelopes, notebook pads, wrapping and artist's papers, waste papers, or any paper product that will adhere with a glue stick

- Minimize noise and the potential for interruptions.
- You may opt to work on this project in more than one sitting.
- If you experience a notable increase in your stress level while doing this project, take a break.
- As you follow directions, be curious and open to what occurs. Refrain from judging the correctness or quality of your artwork and writing.
- If it's comfortable to do so, close your eyes and consciously enjoy three breaths, being aware of the air moving through your nose or the expansion and contraction of your diaphragm.
- Notice where your body is contacting the chair, floor, or table. Look around the room. Experience a sense of being present in your body and surroundings as you begin.

DIRECTIONS

step 1

Look through image sources (listed above in the *PREPARATIONS* section) for a small to medium semi-abstract or realistic image that represents soothing and safety. This image may contain colors, shapes, lines, people, animals, natural or man-made objects, or other visual elements. Cut it out. Place it on your artmaking table where you can readily see it.

If your stress level increases while working on this project, look at this image, consciously breathe, and relax your muscles. Take a moment to notice something in the room or through a window that brings a sense of calmness to you. You may opt to take a break or stop at any time.

step 2

Line up three sheets of white mixed media paper vertically, side-by-side. Tape them together all the way down the seams to make a 27" wide, three-section background.

Trim about an eighth of an inch off the left and right sides of this three-section background panel, so you can readily fold up the background. With the taped side on the back, fold the background inward at the seams, then open it up.

step 3
Briefly note one traumatic event or situation that happened to you in the past. This situation may have occurred over minutes, hours, days, weeks, or years. It may have taken place when you were a child, adolescent, or adult.

Take one or more deep breaths. Consciously relax your muscles if they have tightened.

step 4
More than likely, negative emotional, mental, and/or physical aftereffects will follow a traumatic event or situation. Note any aftereffects you have experienced and are continuing to experience now.

step 5
Select three different, larger-sized found or recycled papers to represent the following:

1. trauma: the traumatic event or situation you identified in step 3
2. aftereffects: the aftereffects you noted in step 4
3. recovery: what it's like or will be like when the aftereffects are less intense, less frequent, or have little or no negative impact on the quality of your life

Why did you specifically choose each of these papers?

step 6

Cut each type of paper you selected into several ¼"- ½" wide strips of any length. These strips do not need to be evenly measured; they can be irregular.

Make three piles of found paper strips: one for trauma, one for aftereffects, and one for recovery.

step 7

On the following pages, there are three consecutive maze pages. Each page represents a different phase of trauma-related experiences.

Notice the increasing amount of white space from the first maze page to the third maze page.

The first page represents the traumatic event or situation, whether it lasted minutes, days, or even years. An arrow marks the entrance to the maze when the trauma began.

The second maze page represents the aftereffects phase.

The third maze page represents the recovery phase that may not have started yet or may be continuing in the present.

In real life, these phases may overlap one another; there may not be a clear demarcation between the phases. A person may also cycle back and forth between these phases.

You can use the provided maze pages, or you may want to draw your own maze on the three-section panel you taped together in step 2. If you're designing your own maze, be sure to have an entrance and at least one exit.

If you want to reuse the provided maze pages at some point, you can photocopy them or trace them onto three sheets of tracing paper and glue those to the white panel you taped together in step 2.

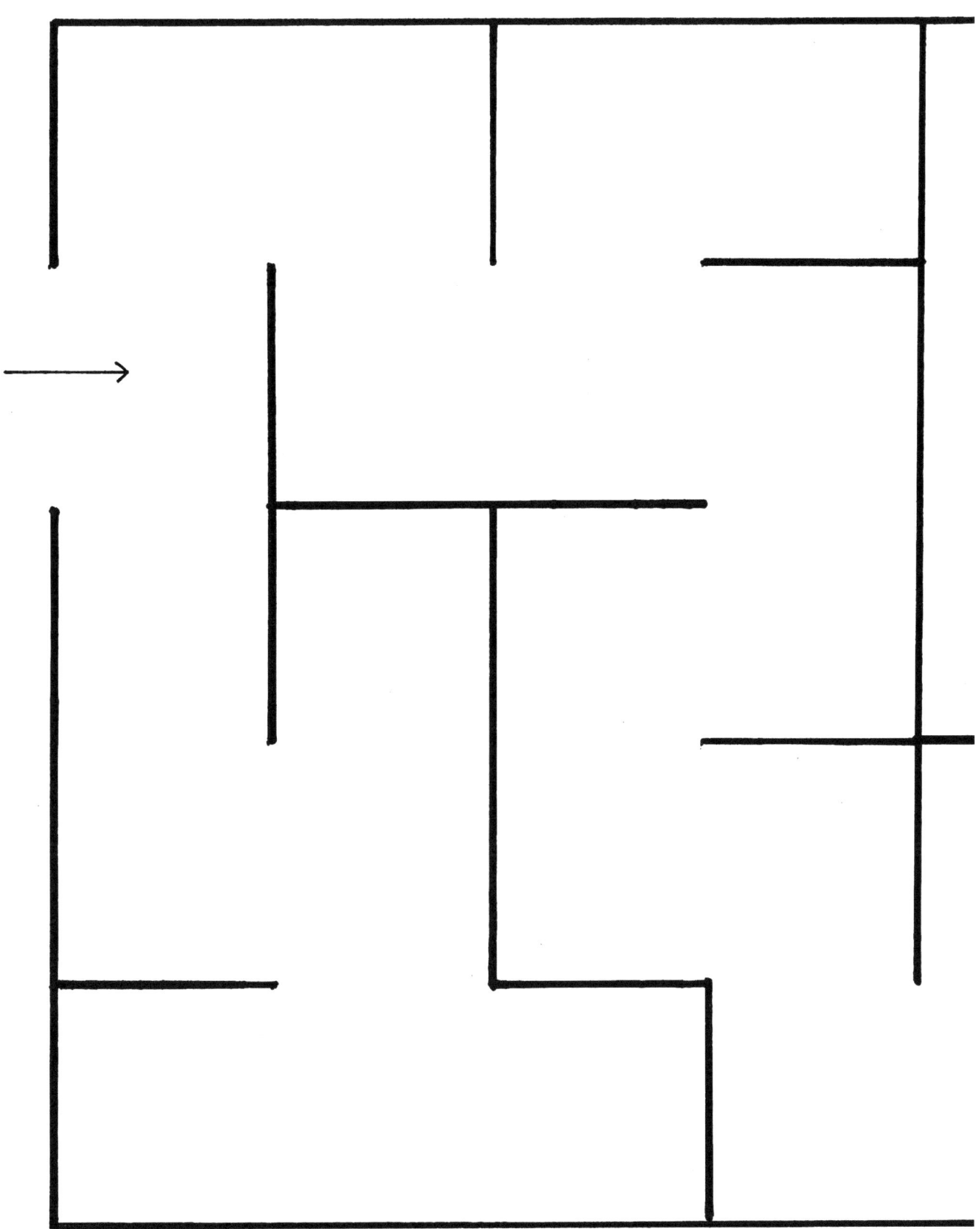

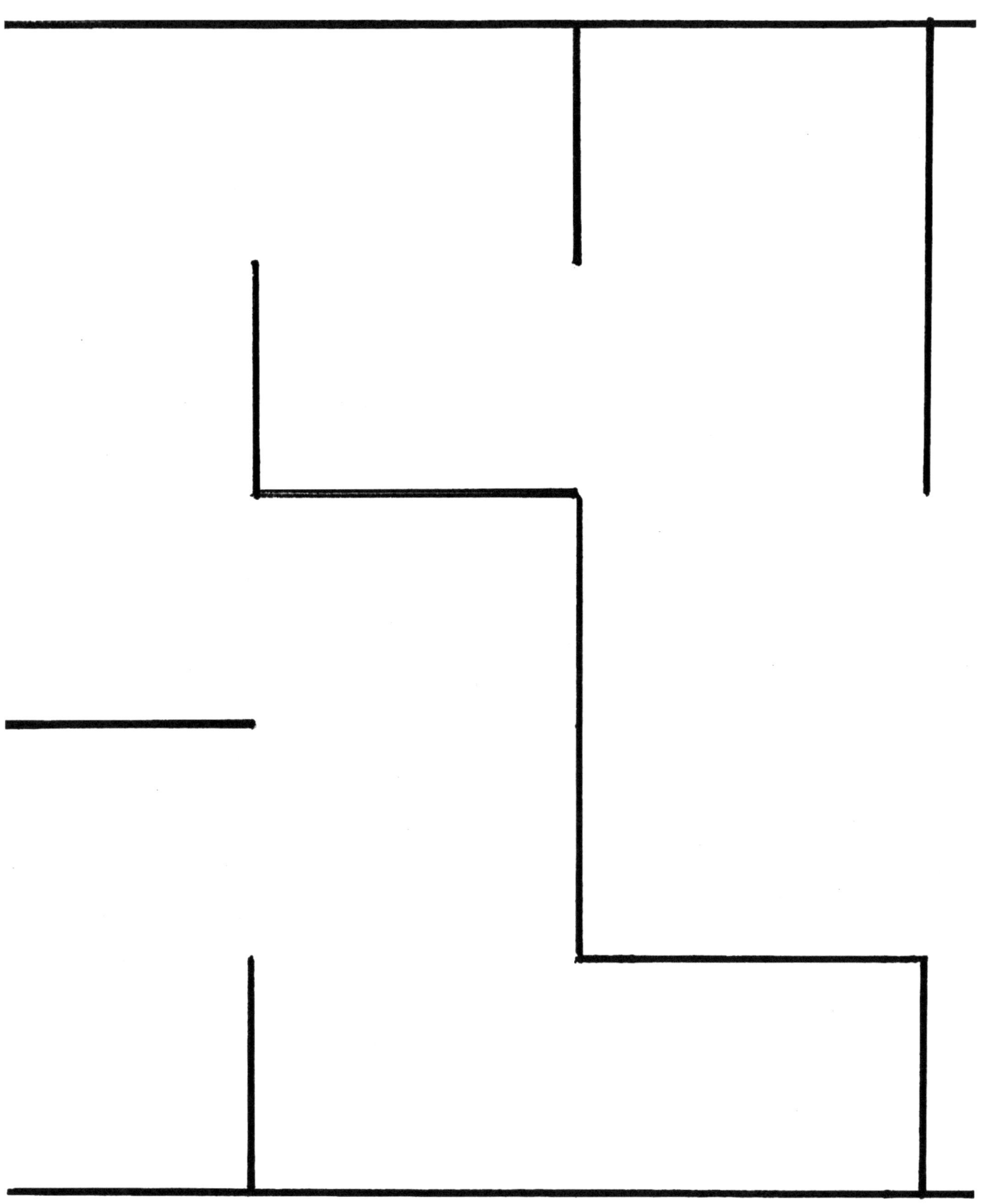

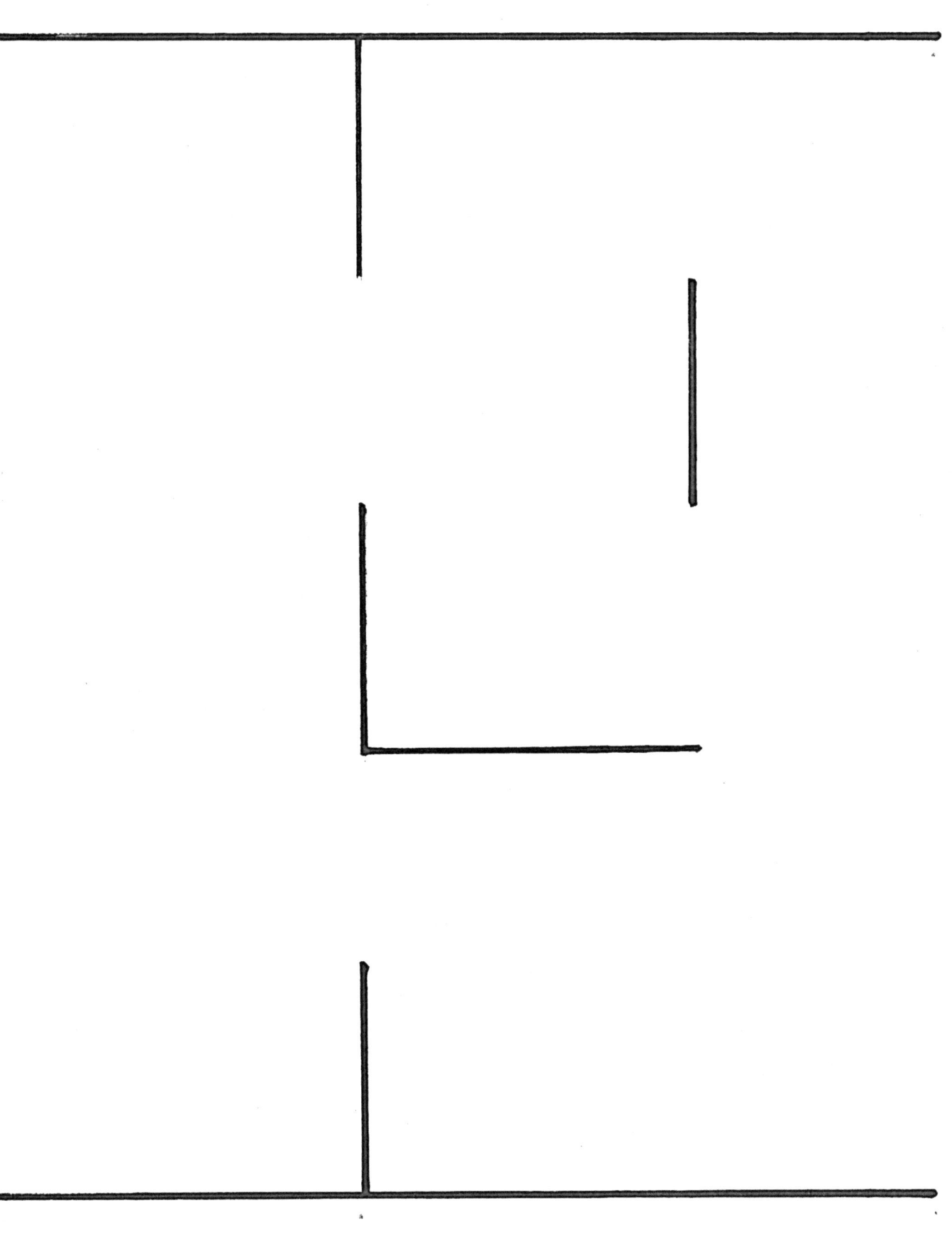

step 8

View the artwork examples at the beginning of this project for a visual reference as you follow the artmaking steps.

Glue the maze pages to the three-section panel in their order, with the trauma section on the left, aftereffects section in the middle, and recovery phase on the right.

Beginning at the entrance of the maze, glue "trauma" paper strips over the maze lines of the first maze section.

In the middle section, glue "aftereffects" strips over the maze lines.

On the last section, glue "recovery" strips over the maze lines.

step 9

Look at your maze. From this present point in time, give compassion to your former self at the time of the trauma. Also give compassion to your previous and current selves for enduring the aftereffects.

- I acknowledge the trauma and aftereffects I've experienced.
- I give myself a kind thought and gesture, such as crossing my arms over my chest, patting my head, or soothing my face and jaws.
- I know that other people in the world have experienced similar trauma and aftereffects; I'm not alone.
- In my mind, I send compassionate thoughts to those people, far and near.

Choose a solid-color paper to represent compassion. What color did you choose? _____

Cut out 3-5 small, simple abstract or symbolic shapes from this paper. Glue them to your maze wherever it's meaningful.

step 10

Circle any personal strengths you may have called on during the trauma and those you're using now to manage any aftereffects.

courage	imagination	open-mindedness	hope	honesty	friendliness	practicality	determination
wisdom	resilience	self-acceptance	faith	integrity	enthusiasm	efficiency	willpower
intuition	endurance	self-regulation	grace	fairness	playfulness	competency	forgiveness
curiosity	adaptability	receiving support	humor	kindness	intelligence	productivity	gratitude
learning	willingness	giving support	energy	devotion	optimism	teamwork	mindfulness
creativity	flexibility	problem-solving	love	patience	spirituality	leadership	humility
bravery	defiance	self-reliance	grit	survival	acceptance	toughness	distraction

Select a solid-color paper to represent these strengths. What color did you choose? _____

Cut out 3-5 small, simple abstract or symbolic shapes from this paper. Glue them to your maze wherever it's meaningful.

step 11

Checkmark or circle any of the following wellbeing strategies that will help you manage the aftereffects of the trauma. (See Appendix A, page 290, for a detailed description of these practices.)

PHYSICAL SELF-CARE: Attend to your nutrition and hydration, exercise, sleep routine, and physical and dental checkups. Follow through with recommendations from health providers.

SELF CHECK-IN: Identify your emotions. Determine your state of mind. Do a quick body scan. Are you relatively ok in the present moment? If not, what do you need to attend to?

PAUSE / GO SLOWER: Take a breath. Be aware of inhaling and exhaling. Consciously relax tense muscles.

PRESENT MOMENT AWARENESS: Be in the present moment, whether it's pleasant, neutral, or unpleasant. Be aware of what you see, hear, smell, taste, and touch. Acknowledge your thoughts and feelings. Allow them to pass through your mind and body without pushing them away or clinging to them.

COMPASSION: Acknowledge a problem or difficulty. Give a caring, kind thought and/or gesture to yourself. Know other people in the world are experiencing something similar; you're not alone. In your mind, send compassionate thoughts to those people, far and near.

MULTI-PERSPECTIVES: Look at any given situation from more than one point of view. See the bigger picture.

GRATITUDE: Take time to appreciate what is good in your life. Take care of your life. Take care of what you value in your life.

POSITIVE EXPERIENCES: Be aware of positive experiences while they're happening. Create more enjoyable moments in your everyday life.

SELF-ACCEPTANCE / SELF-VALIDATION: Accept your vulnerabilities, imperfections, talents, skills, and strengths without comparing yourself to others.

VALUES: Circle a few values below that are most meaningful to you. Live by them each day.

family	service	success	wisdom	balance	teamwork
friendship	peace	equality	joy	integrity	knowledge
marriage	freedom	prestige	play	bravery	education
commitment	responsibility	career	humor	mental health	recreation
parenting	security	diversity	beauty	physical health	religion
pets	loyalty	generosity	honesty	physical fitness	spirituality
community	justice	love	trust	relaxation	authenticity
nature	creativity	faith	gratitude	meditation	adventure
safety	home	comfort	job	ethical behavior	financial security

MEDITATIVE FOCUS / CONTEMPLATION: If possible, engage in meditation, yoga, tai chi, qigong, prayer, spiritual study, or another inspirational or contemplative practice each day.

DAILY RECAP: Review a difficult moment. Determine what made it difficult. What can you learn from this? What small choice did you make today to reduce stress or create a positive experience? What are you most grateful for today?

Select one solid-color paper to represent the wellbeing practices you checked or circled.

What color did you choose? _____
Cut out 3-5 small, simple abstract or symbolic shapes from this paper. Glue them to your maze wherever it's meaningful.

step 12

List any supportive people or organizations that have been helpful to you in dealing with the trauma and any additional ones that can be helpful as you continue to move forward.

_____

_____

_____

_____

_____

Select a solid-color paper to represent these supports.

What color did you choose? _____

Cut 1-5 small, simple abstract or symbolic shapes from this paper. Glue them to your maze wherever it's meaningful.

step 13

Glue the soothing image you cut out in step 1 to your maze, wherever it seems most appropriate to do so.

step 14

Consider your future recovery process. Even if you're continuing to experience a significant level of aftereffects from the trauma, imagine what your re-envisioned life might be like when the aftereffects become less intense, less frequent, or disappear. You'll be writing your thoughts on the next page. Feel free to write in any style and form that is preferable to you.

Following are two examples of writing from other artmakers who have previously completed this project.

I am no longer boxed in like before. Like a lion released from a cage, I can look out and up and view things happening now, not overly colored by what I've experienced in the past. I'm more confident and able to speak, to support myself in a balanced way. Even though my path is sometimes steep and curved, I walk the middle of the road, looking from side to side and ahead to see the clear energy that surrounds me. I am free to look in the direction of what is important to me and what will keep me safe while enjoying my life.

The maze no longer entraps me.
I have flown above.
Lightness of being.
I walk with wisdom, grace, and hope.
The trauma will always be with me.
It is part of my history
But it no longer stops me,
No longer tells me
What I cannot do or be.
I see only possibilities now.
Look for beauty in all things.

You may want to answer the following questions in your writing:

What will it be like for me as I gain distance and time from the maze?
Will I see, hear, feel, think, or act differently?

Be as specific as possible. If you'd like, use any of the following words or phrases in your writing.

relief	progress	opportunity	openness	flexibility	breath of fresh air
hope	release	possibility	confidence	peace	lightness of being
safety	time	clarity	new frontier	sky	greater sense of space
grace	gratitude	comfort	more choices	liberation	full swing
agility	dignity	security	pleasantries	beauty	increased wellbeing
freedom	healthier	happier	enjoyment	kinder	more contented
simpler	mindful	open	acceptance	creative	better balanced
alive	self-trust	relief	compassion	approval	self-acceptance

Read your writing out loud so you can both see and hear it.

LIFE APPLICATIONS

- Following a traumatic event or situation, physical self-care is vital. Adequate nutrition, hydration, exercise, and sleep routines will help to reduce the aftereffects. What is one way you can realistically boost your physical self-care routine now?

  _____

  _____

- When you're experiencing more intense emotional, mental, physical, or behavioral aftereffects, consider practicing one or more of the following ways to manage your stress:

  Ground in present moment awareness by tapping your feet on the floor and naming objects you see in your environment.

  Acknowledge your inhalations and exhalations, repeating to yourself, "breathing in, breathing out."

  Drink a glass of water or other health-giving liquid. Focus on picking up a glass or cup, slowly pouring the liquid, refreshing your mouth, tasting, and swallowing each sip.

  Consciously relax your muscles, starting with your head and face and moving down to your toes.

  Use distraction to disengage from intense unpleasant thoughts or emotions. For example, walk outside while noticing what you see and hear, watch a fun video or movie, play with a pet, listen to soothing music, dance, practice tai chi, qigong, yoga, or engage in another physical activity.

- You can revisit your art and writing from this project if their messages and insights can benefit your ongoing recovery.

CONCLUSIONS

- Note any useful insights, revelations, beliefs, or intentions that emerged while you worked on this project or that come to mind now.

  _____

  _____

  _____

- Detect any tension you're holding in your neck, shoulders, or elsewhere in your body. Consciously relax, pat, massage, or gently stretch those areas.
- If it's comfortable to do so, close your eyes and consciously enjoy three breaths.
- Notice where your body is contacting the chair, floor, or table. Look around the room. Experience a sense of being present in your body and surroundings as you finish.
- Sign and date your artwork. Store it for safekeeping.

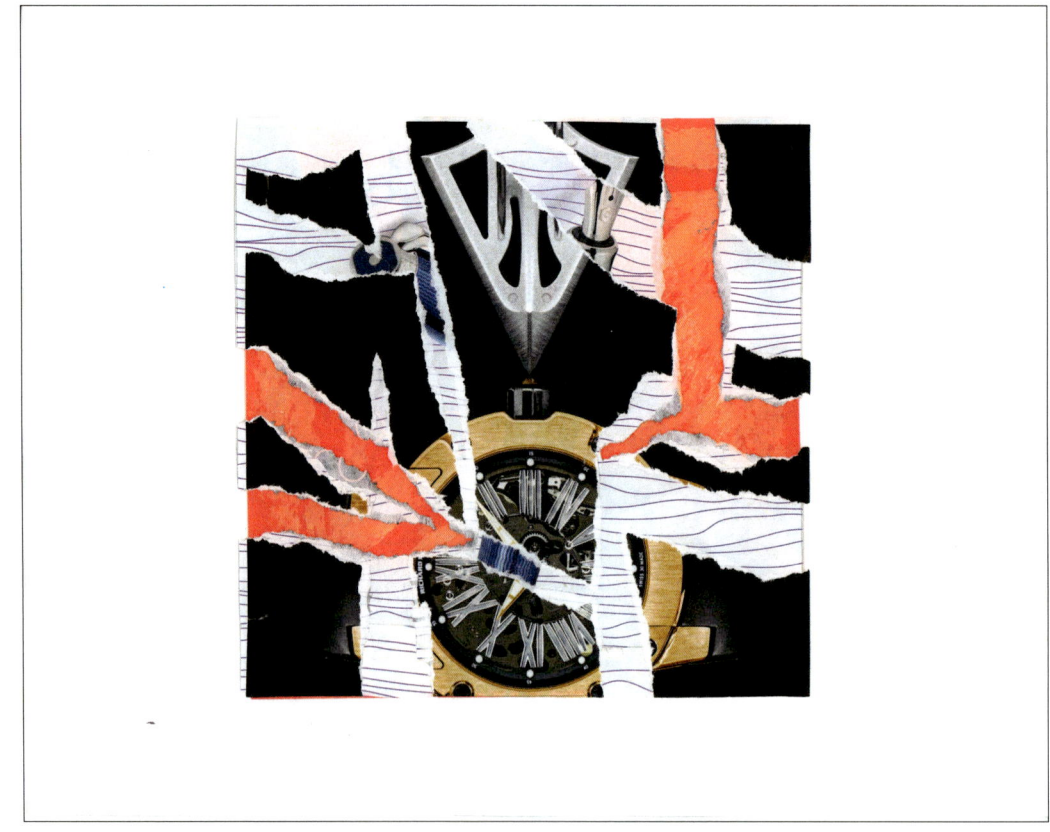

project 15

PEEL BACK THE LAYERS
anger & vulnerability

At times, all human beings feel anger ranging from mild annoyance to serious rage. Anger can also manifest as jealousy, resentment, defiance, and rebellion. When we're over stressed, anger often results. It serves the purpose of letting us know we may need to investigate a problem or make a change. Unfortunately, anger often goes hand-in-hand with casting blame on others or ourselves.

Anger poses the potential for harm when it's suppressed, extremely intense, or leads to actions that make our lives worse or hurt others. If we don't pay attention to our anger, it may develop into a chronic state of toxic stress, hostility, and depression. If this happens, anger is no longer a response to what is happening in the present; it becomes a constant way of being and acting in the world.

Instead of letting anger build-up through avoidance or denial, we can safely acknowledge and express our anger while exploring the underlying conditions and feelings. With increased understanding, we can offer ourselves compassion, then decide if there is something we need to do to address the situation in a productive way without fueling more anger or blame.

Through art and writing, you'll identify one event or situation that is giving rise to anger and acknowledge emotions and conditions that may be hidden underneath your anger. You'll layer two found images on top of a solid-color piece of paper and peel off strips of the images, deconstructing your artwork to reveal the color of self-compassion. If you choose to do so, you'll compose a fill-in-the-blanks poem that refers to your artwork.

PREPARATIONS

- Clear and protect the surface of your artmaking table.
- Gather tools and materials: pen or pencil for writing
    ruler
    scissors
    glue stick
    9"x12" white mixed media paper, 1 sheet
    GLOSSY found images from used magazines or other sources
    8½"x11" or 9"x12" assorted solid-color papers
    watch, clock, or timer

- Minimize noise and the potential for interruptions.
- You may opt to work on this project in more than one sitting.
- If you experience a notable increase in your stress level while doing this project, take a break.
- As you follow directions, be curious and open to what occurs. Refrain from judging the correctness or quality of your artwork and writing.
- If it's comfortable to do so, close your eyes and consciously enjoy three breaths, being aware of the air moving through your nose or the expansion and contraction of your diaphragm.
- Notice where your body is contacting the chair, floor, or table. Look around the room. Experience a sense of being present in your body and surroundings as you begin.

DIRECTIONS

step 1
Describe something in your life that brings a sense of calm and peace to you.

step 2
Describe a recent event, ongoing situation, or something else that is activating irritation or anger in you. What, when, where, who?

Specify whether this anger is directed toward self, other(s), circumstances, the world, or something else.

_____
_____
_____

step 3
Circle 1-2 words that best describe the level or kind of anger you're feeling:

annoyance	resentment	ill-tempered	vexation	frustration	aggravation
dislike	irritation	disgust	bitterness	revenge	displeasure
impatience	rage	testiness	hostility	exasperation	infuriation
hatred	defiance	jealousy	indignation	disagreement	rebellion

Is your anger mild, moderate, serious, or severe? _____

How long have you felt anger related to the specific situation you described in step 2? _____

Has the degree of your anger gotten worse, better, stayed the same, or does it fluctuate over time?

_____

Where do you feel this anger in your body? _____

step 4
Look through magazines or other sources of **glossy** images for an abstract, semi-abstract, or realistic image to represent how your anger feels to you. This image needs to be at least 6"x 6" and may contain colors, shapes, lines, people, animals, indoor or outdoor scenes, natural or man-made objects, art reproductions, or other visual elements.

Trim this image to measure 6"x 6".

Look closely at the image. Describe it below.

_____
_____
_____
_____

step 5

To look deeper into your anger, consider the following feelings and conditions that may underlie the anger you described in step 2. Circle 2-5 words that best apply.

fear	helplessness	sadness	gloom
uncertainty	worry	grief	unhappiness
doubt	anxiety	heartbrokenness	misery
dread	stress	hopelessness	disgust
insecurity	panic	resignation	regret
vulnerability	desperation	disappointment	shame or guilt
terror	illness	discouragement	invalidation
threat	pain	confusion	hurt
exhaustion	boredom	failure	loss
rejection	overlooked	being ignored	underappreciated
victimized	manipulated	cheated	taken advantage of

step 6

Look through magazines or other sources of **glossy** images for an abstract, semi-abstract, or realistic image to represent one or more words you circled in step 5. This image needs to be at least 6"x 6" and may contain colors, shapes, lines, people, animals, indoor or outdoor scenes, natural or man-made objects, art reproductions, or other visual elements.

Trim this image to measure 6"x 6".

Look closely at this image. Describe it below.

_____

_____

_____

_____

step 7

Look at both images you chose from steps 4 and 6. Practice self-compassion.

1. I acknowledge how stressful it is to feel anger and the underlying emotions or conditions.
2. I give myself a kind thought and/or gesture, such as taking a conscious breath, massaging my jaw, or exercising.
3. I know other people in the world are experiencing similar anger and underlying emotions and conditions; I'm not alone.
4. In my mind, I send compassionate thoughts to those people, far and near.

Choose a solid-color paper to represent self-compassion. Cut this paper to measure 6"x 6".

step 8

Read the following artmaking instructions before proceeding. You'll be layering the 6"x 6" squares on top of each other. View the artwork examples at the beginning of this project for a visual reference.

1. Glue the solid-color self-compassion square to the middle of a sheet of white mixed media paper.
2. Apply glue quickly over the entire top of that solid-color square.
3. Place the "underlying emotion/condition" image from step 6 on top of the glue.
4. Quickly apply glue over the entire top of that image.
5. Place the "anger" image from step 4 on top of the glue.
6. Wait 4-5 minutes. (It's best not to wait any longer, as it will be difficult to peel the strips.)

While you're waiting, you might want to take a few conscious breaths, relax your muscles starting at the top of your head down to your toes, look around the room or out a window to see something pleasant, or review your writing in step 1.

7. Loosen a part of the edge of only the top image with your fingernail or scissors tip.
8. Tear off a strip of that image to reveal a portion of the underlying image. Repeat, peeling off 1 or 2 more strips.
9. Loosen a part of the edge of the top layer along with the edge of the second layer image. Peel off 2-3 strips of the combined top and second layer to reveal some of the solid-color square underneath.

Look at your artwork. What do you notice?

_____

_____

Pile the peeled strips together. Can you look at this pile as a symbol of beginning to let go of your anger and underlying feelings or conditions?

step 9

In this step you'll be composing a fill-in-the-blanks poem related to your artwork. Following are two examples of writing from other artmakers who have previously completed this project.

PEELING AWAY FROM RAGE

Affixed to one another, layers of resentment along with jealousy. I peel away strips of fire filling a forest, destroying all life in its path, along with shreds of criticism, abandonment and loss, and dregs of a tattered sense of self. I am alone, falling off a cliff, towards the turbulent water. I do not want to drown. And here, once hidden from view, compassion rises to the surface right before my eyes.

DECONSTRUCTED ANGER

*Affixed to one another, layers of irritation and helplessness
along with dread weighing heavily on my breath and mind. I peel away
strips of neon and disconnected dots. I detach shreds and dregs of delay,
pulling off a tattered past while I wait for a lift to the top of a snow-covered
mountain. And now, right before my eyes, compassion rises
to the surface to ease and comfort my being.*

Fill in the following blanks to create your poem. Use the provided prompts beneath the blanks. Change the tense or form of your words if needed.

_____
(title)

Affixed to one another, layers of _____
(Fill in this blank with 1-2 words you circled in step 3.)

along with _____ .
(Fill in this blank with 1 word you circled in step 5)

I peel away strips of _____
(Fill in this blank and the following blank with words & phrases you wrote in step 4)

_____ ,

I detach shreds and dregs of _____ ,
(Fill in this blank with other words from step 5.)

pulling off tattered _____
(Fill in this blank and the following blank with words & phrases you wrote in step 6.)

_____ .

And now, right before my eyes, compassion rises to the surface to ease and comfort my being.

Read your writing out loud so you can both see and hear it.

If you wish, feel free to change the order, add other words or phrases, and make other revisions. You may want to write or type your poem on a separate sheet of paper and give it a title.

LIFE APPLICATIONS

- When you become aware that intense or deep anger is on the rise, pause or take a timeout before speaking or acting. Take a breath. Relax your muscles. If you're with another person or a group of people who are involved in your anger, leave the room or immediate area to avoid escalation.

- If at any time you think your anger may be nearing the potential for physical harm, immediately call or have someone else call your local or national emergency phone number.

- It's essential to understand and deal with anger in a positive way. Ask yourself the following questions. Write your answers on a separate sheet of paper.

    1. Is my anger serving to motivate or protect me in some way? If so, how?

    2. Are my anger and underlying feelings/conditions linked to something else in the past? Can I break that link to the past now?

    3. Anger can intensify with hunger, fatigue, and excessive alcohol or drug use. Do I need to attend to any of these factors?

    4. Can I look at my anger and underlying feelings/conditions from a different point of view? If so, what is that point of view?

    5. Without placing blame on others or myself, what is my anger trying to tell me?

    6. Does this anger or do underlying emotions/conditions indicate a need for change? Do I need to take any positive actions or activate wellbeing practices (see page 260) to deal responsibly with my anger and underlying emotions/conditions?

    7. How can I express this anger calmly, using "I" statements without criticizing or blaming someone else?

    8. What can I do to make the situation better or to accept what has happened and make the best of the situation?

CONCLUSIONS

- Note any useful insights, revelations, beliefs, or intentions that emerged while you worked on this project or that come to mind now.

- Detect any tension you're holding in your neck, shoulders, or elsewhere in your body. Consciously relax, pat, massage, or gently stretch those areas.
- If it's comfortable to do so, close your eyes and consciously enjoy three breaths.
- Notice where your body is contacting the chair, floor, or table. Look around the room. Experience a sense of being present in your body and surroundings as you finish.
- Sign and date your artwork. Store it for safekeeping.

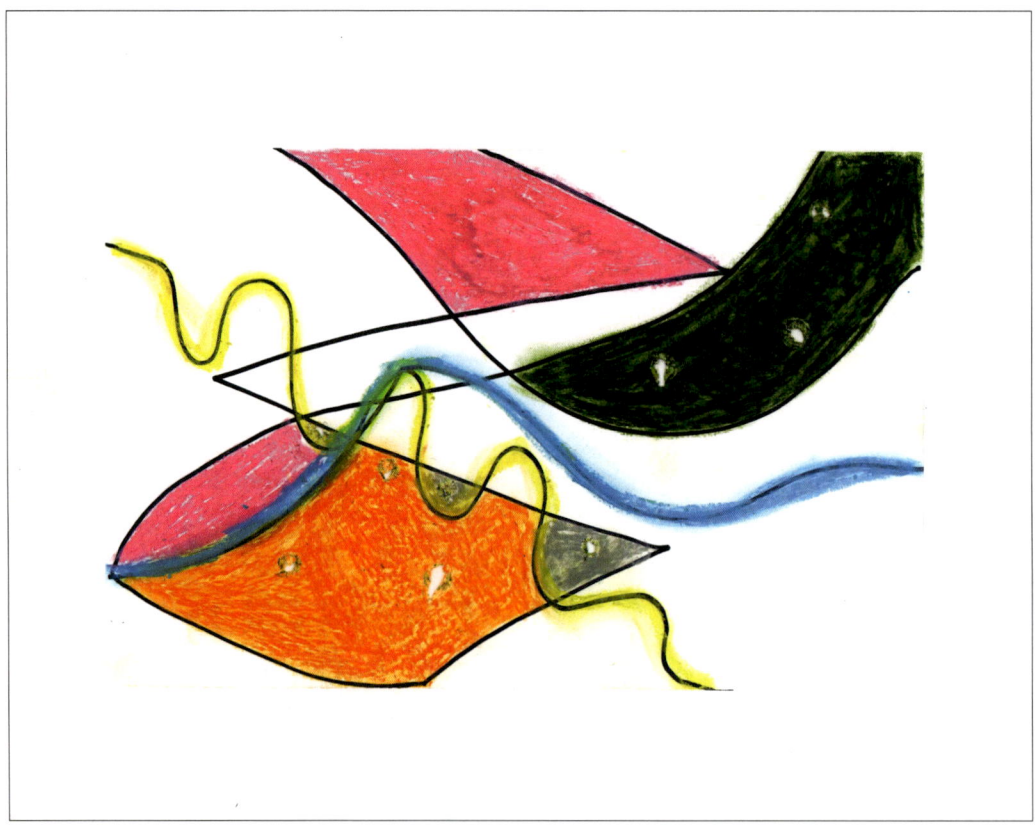

project **16**

PUNCH HOLES IN YOUR PAINFUL PAST
shame & guilt

Shame and guilt are social, self-conscious emotions that keep us in line with cultural norms and our own values. Yet, when we chronically feel shame and guilt, they become entrenched in our way of being, generating stress, low self-worth, depression, isolation, and self-impairing behaviors. When shame and guilt are related to trauma, they may last long after the actual traumatic events have occurred.

The terms, *shame* and *guilt*, are often used interchangeably, but there are differences between them. They share some of the same networks in our brains but not all. Shame occurs when we believe there is something fundamentally wrong with us as human beings. It can arise when other people reject or abuse us or when we don't meet certain cultural or group standards that we think are essential to our self-image.

Guilt is related to our behaviors. It indicates that we believe we've done something that has caused harm to others, the environment, or ourselves. It goes beyond simple regret that is experienced as mild sadness or disappointment into a deeper distress that is accompanied by the wish that whatever happened wouldn't have occurred. The need to apologize or make amends are associated with guilt.

Shame is feeling bad about our core selves. Guilt is feeling bad about our behaviors. Some situations may cause us to feel both shame and guilt simultaneously. This occurs when we believe we're basically inadequate as human beings and we've acted in hurtful ways.

In this project, artmaking starts with a simple abstract line drawing. You'll use oil pastels to color some of the interior abstract shapes, then proceed to punch holes in the shame and/or guilt shapes. You'll answer questions to explore the origins of your shame and/or guilt.

If you're working with shame, you'll work toward freeing yourself from its hold through understanding and self-compassion. If you're working with guilt, you'll generate ideas for acts of atonement that will allow you to begin forgiving yourself for your wrongdoing. If you choose to do so, you'll write a fill-in-the-blanks poem related to the meaning of your artwork.

PREPARATIONS

- Clear and protect the surface of your artmaking table.
- Gather tools and materials: pen or pencil for writing
  scissors
  glue stick
  9"x12" sheet of white mixed media paper, 2 sheets
  chisel-tip marker
  oil pastels
  paper towel

- Minimize noise and the potential for interruptions.
- You may opt to work on this project in more than one sitting.
- If you experience a notable increase in your stress level while doing this project, take a break.
- As you follow directions, be curious and open to what occurs. Refrain from judging the correctness or quality of your artwork and writing.
- If it's comfortable to do so, close your eyes and consciously enjoy three breaths, being aware of the air moving through your nose or the expansion and contraction of your diaphragm.
- Notice where your body is contacting the chair, floor, or table. Look around the room. Experience a sense of being present in your body and surroundings as you begin.

DIRECTIONS

step 1
On the following blank lines, note 1-3 of your qualities, skills, talents, or strengths from the list below that make you feel good about yourself.

_____

_____

courage	imagination	open-mindedness	hope	honesty	friendliness	practicality	determination
wisdom	resilience	self-acceptance	faith	integrity	enthusiasm	efficiency	willpower
intuition	endurance	self-regulation	grace	fairness	playfulness	competency	forgiveness
curiosity	adaptability	receiving support	humor	kindness	intelligence	productivity	gratitude
learning	willingness	giving support	energy	devotion	optimism	teamwork	mindfulness
creativity	flexibility	problem-solving	love	patience	spirituality	leadership	humility

step 2
Briefly describe one event or situation from the recent or more distant past that continues to cause you to feel shame and/or guilt when it comes to mind.

_____

_____

_____

step 3

Differentiate between whether this event or situation is causing you to feel shame (thinking you're fundamentally inadequate, defective, or damaged) or guilt (you've acted wrongly or haven't acted when you needed to). Or you may feel both shame and guilt related to the event or situation you described in step 2.

Circle any of the following words or phrases that apply to your shame and/or guilt regarding the event or situation you described in step 2.

IF YOU'RE FEELING <u>SHAME</u> (self-worth related)   **I see myself as . . .**

not good enough	dysfunctional	unworthy	defective	damaged	weak
a disappointment	unacceptable	defiled	an outsider	worthless	pitiful
less than others	messed-up	a failure	too needy	inadequate	a loser
beyond repair	unlovable	pathetic	unlikeable	unsuccessful	stupid

IF YOU'RE FEELING <u>GUILT</u> (behavior related)   **I . . .**

caused harm to myself	gravely misbehaved	harmed someone or something
invalidated someone	seriously acted out	spoke badly about someone
made a bad mistake	humiliated someone	betrayed someone
was mean	did wrong	didn't act when I should have
bullied someone	neglected something	abandoned someone
shirked responsibility	reacted inappropriately	avoided someone or something
overstepped boundaries	avoided an obligation	survived when others perished

step 4

If you're working with shame, consider the possibility that something earlier in your life may be contributing to the shame you feel now. Shame often originates from a source outside of you, from other people's remarks or behaviors toward you, or from cultural or group standards that you couldn't meet for one reason or another.

You may have been abused, bullied, neglected, passed over, treated as if you didn't matter, abandoned, or invalidated. Shame can also be related to physical or mental disabilities or differences in how we act or speak.

What previous factors may be contributing to the shame you identified in step 2?

_____

_____

_____

By acknowledging when and how your shame may have originated, you can understand that you're probably not to blame for having this feeling. This is a step toward breaking free of shame and learning to feel compassion for yourself.

If you're working with guilt, it's beneficial to understand what may have contributed to your harmful actions or inactions. This knowledge may prevent similar wrongdoings in the future. What circumstances or influences led to your wrongdoing as it relates to the event or situation you described in step 2?

_____

_____

_____

How did these circumstances, influences, or something else from the past contribute to your wrongdoing?

_____

_____

_____

_____

step 5

View the artwork examples at the beginning of this project for a visual reference as you follow the artmaking steps.

Cut one sheet of white mixed media paper in half. In this step you'll be using a chisel-tip marker to draw five lines on one of the half-sheets of paper. These lines can be straight, diagonal, curved, wavy, angular, or a mix of types of lines. Your lines may look different from the ones drawn in the artwork examples. Let your lines randomly intersect one another.

Draw the following five lines:

1. a line from the top edge of the paper to the bottom edge
2. a line from the left edge to the right edge of the paper
3. a line from the top to one side of the paper
4. a line from the bottom to one side of the paper
5. a line from the right edge to the left edge

step 6

At times you may feel as if you've lost your basic goodness or worthiness due to imperfections, harmful things that have happened to you, or because of mistakes you have made. Even though your basic goodness may sometimes seem obscured, it remains a part of you.

Choose an oil pastel color to represent your basic goodness. What color did you choose? _____

Apply this color on top of one of the black lines so you can see goodness running through your artwork. Rub a small piece of clean paper towel over this color line to smooth it.

step 7

Look back at step 1. Select one of your qualities, skills, talents, or strengths that might help you manage your shame and/or guilt.

Which one did you choose? _____

Pick another oil pastel color to represent this positive self-aspect. What color did you pick? _____

Apply this color over one of the black lines so you can see this positive self-aspect running through your artwork. Rub a small piece of clean paper towel over this color line to smooth it.

step 8

Choose 1-2 oil pastel colors to represent the shame and/or guilt you described in step 2.

What color(s) did you choose? _____

Look at your artwork in progress. The lines you have drawn can be seen as outlines of interior white shapes. Color in 1-3 white shapes with the color(s) you just selected for shame and/or guilt. Try not to color over your basic goodness or positive self-aspect lines.

Rub a small piece of clean paper towel over these shapes to smooth the colors.

step 9

Over long periods of time, extreme shame and guilt can overshadow a positive sense of self.

Color in 1-2 white shapes with gray oil pastel to represent this overshadowing.

step 10

Practicing self-compassion can help relieve the effects of shame and guilt.

1. I acknowledge the difficulty of feeling shame and/or guilt.
2. I offer compassion to myself by way of a kind thought and/or gesture, such as touching my shoulder, soothing my forehead, or hugging myself.
3. I know other people in the world are experiencing similar shame and/or guilt; I'm not alone.
4. In my mind, I send compassionate thoughts to those people, far and near.

Choose an oil pastel color to represent self-compassion. What color did you choose? _____
Color in 2-5 white shapes with this color.

Rub a small piece of clean paper towel over these shapes to smooth the color.

Where do you feel shame or guilt in your body? _____

In your mind, send the color you chose for self-compassion to those parts of your body.

step 11

Once the worst of your shame or guilt has lifted, what improvement will result? Circle 1-5 of the following words to describe the results.

clarity	calmness	self-forgiveness	resolution	alleviation	solace
sanity	comfort	forgiveness	amelioration	appeasement	restoration
peace	release	my truer humanity	softening	abatement	reconciliation
relief	composure	self-acceptance	integrity	dignity	wholeness
honor	truthfulness	self-trust	wellbeing	atonement	self-respect

Choose an oil pastel color to represent the words you circled. What color did you choose? _____

Color in 1-3 white shapes with this color.

Rub a small piece of clean paper towel over this color to smooth it.

step 12

In your artwork, locate the shame and/or guilt-colored shapes as well as the gray overshadowing shapes.

With the pointed end of a pencil or pen, punch several holes in these shapes. Punch through the paper until each hole is the diameter of the pencil or pen. Be careful not to puncture your fingers.

From the backside of the paper, fold back any paper hanging from the holes, so the holes are wide open.

step 13

Apply glue to the back of your artwork. Center it on a white sheet of mixed media paper, making sure the holes are wide open. Use a clean sheet of paper on top of your artwork to press and flatten your artwork onto the surface of the white background paper.

Look at your artwork from arm's length. By acknowledging your shame and/or guilt, giving it air and light, and practicing self-compassion, you can sense the burden of the shame or guilt you described in step 2 is lifting.

If it's comfortable to do so, gently straighten your upper body, roll your shoulders in a backward motion one or two times. Open your chest outward. Get in touch with your right to be who you are and take your rightful place in the world. Look up and out.

step 14

In this step you'll be composing a fill-in-the-blanks poem related to the meaning of your artwork. Following are two examples of poems written by artmakers who previously completed this project.

LETTING GO, LOOKING AHEAD

Punch holes in the past, in the livelihood lost.
Give air to the burden of seeing myself as unworthy.
Give light to the overshadowing of humiliation and loss.
Acknowledge the origins behind the guilt.
Reinstate my rightful goodness, my goodful rightness.
Reinforce my sky blue sightline to run the distance.
Reinfuse my green guidelines to keep the course.
Let me go forward with dignity.

ENOUGH ANGUISH

Probe, press, poke, then pierce the surface of shame.
Punch holes in the past. Give air to scars of humiliation.
Give light to the overshadowing of disgust and damage.
To run the distance, I reinstate my rightful self-worth
and reinforce my bright yellow sightline.
To keep the course, I reinvest in my musical talents.
I reinfuse my courage and determination. From here on,
I go forward with self-respect and resolution.

Compose your poem on the following page using the provided prompts below the blank lines. If you wish, write or type, and revise your poem on a separate sheet of paper.

_____
(title)

Probe, press, poke, then pierce the paper's surface.

Punch holes in the past, in the _____
(Fill in these blanks with words or phrases you wrote in step 2.)

_____ .

Give air to the burden of seeing myself as _____ .
(Fill in the above blank with 1 or more words or phrases you circled in step 3.)

Give light to the overshadowing of _____ .
(Fill in the above blank with the word *shame* and/or *guilt*.)

To run the distance, I reinstate my rightful goodness; reinforce my _____
(Fill in the above blank with the color you named in step 6.)

*sightline. To keep the course , I reinform and reinfuse my*_____.
(Fill in the above blank with circled or written words from step 1.)

From here on, I choose to go forward with _____ .
(Fill in the above blank with 1 or more words you circled in step 10.)

Feel free to change the tense or form of words, revise the order, and add or delete words and phrases. Give your poem a title.

Read your poem out loud so you can both see and hear it.

LIFE APPLICATIONS

- What is one thing you would do differently if your shame and/or guilt were significantly diminished or entirely gone?

  _____

- If you're working with shame, what is one way you could live more authentically once the shame has lifted?

  _____

- If you're working with guilt, identify at least one way you can make reparations for what you did or didn't do. If it's impossible to directly apologize or make amends to a person or to something in the environment you have harmed, you can atone by doing something good in the world. For instance, you could contribute time, effort, or money to a related cause or be helpful to someone in some associated way.

  _____

  _____

  If you have treated yourself badly, how can you compassionately make amends to yourself?

  _____

As adults, it's important for us to take responsibility for wrongdoings, no matter what the cause. When you have made amends appropriate to the level of harm you have caused, you can begin to forgive yourself, whether others have forgiven you or not.

CONCLUSIONS

- Note any useful insights, revelations, beliefs, or intentions that emerged while you worked on this project or that come to mind now.

  _____

  _____

  _____

- Detect any tension you're holding in your neck, shoulders, or elsewhere in your body. Consciously relax, pat, massage, or gently stretch those areas.
- If it's comfortable to do so, close your eyes and consciously enjoy three breaths.
- Notice where your body is contacting the chair, floor, or table. Look around the room. Experience a sense of being present in your body and surroundings as you finish.
- Sign and date your artwork. Store it for safekeeping.

project 17

WALK THROUGH A WALL OF FEAR

courage & determination

No one is exempt from fear; it's hard-wired into our brains to serve as an alarm that protects us from real or perceived harm, whether that threat is physical or psychological. Low-level fear can sharpen our senses and help us prepare for challenges, whereas high-level fear may dull our senses and impair our ability to think, function, or act.

Responses to fear include flight, fight, freeze, crying for help, and submitting to or pleasing someone to avoid maltreatment. Any of these responses may serve to protect us during ongoing or imminently threatening situations, but if continued after the initial danger has passed, they may lead to chronic stress, self-doubt, frustration, confusion, and helplessness. We may end up feeling diminished, depressed, or oppressed.

Fear can be compared to a wall that keeps us from fully living our lives. When we find ways to understand and normalize our fear, we can focus more on creating our lives and less on what we fear. We can gather enough courage and determination to keep the door of possibility open and take the risk of walking through the wall. We may find that we're rewarded for our bravery with new opportunities in unexpected ways.

To represent your wall of fear, you'll select one of the provided wall photos and cut a door in this photo, allowing you to see through to an image representing a positive possibility on the other side of the wall. You'll add colored shapes to represent strengths and supports and write instructions or compose an instruction poem that provides guidance to face and walk through the wall with more assurance.

PREPARATIONS

- Clear and protect the surface of your artmaking table.
- Gather tools and materials: pencil and eraser
  scissors
  glue stick
  9"x12" white mixed media paper, 1 sheet
  8½"x11" or 9"x12" assorted solid-color papers
  tape (optional)
  image sources, such as used magazines, books, newspapers, brochures, catalogs, old calendars, greeting cards, photocopies, online printouts, your own photos

- Minimize noise and the potential for interruptions.
- You may opt to work on this project in more than one sitting.
- If you experience a notable increase in your stress level while doing this project, take a break.
- As you follow directions, be curious and open to what occurs. Refrain from judging the correctness or quality of your artwork and writing.
- If it's comfortable to do so, close your eyes and consciously enjoy three breaths, being aware of the air moving through your nose or the expansion and contraction of your diaphragm.
- Notice where your body is contacting the chair, floor, or table. Look around the room. Experience a sense of being present in your body and surroundings as you begin.

DIRECTIONS

step 1

Visualize a real or imaginary safe place where you feel little or no fear. This could be a sanctuary, retreat, or restful vacation spot. Imagine yourself in this place. Is it inside or outside? Describe what you see, hear, smell, and touch. What is the temperature? Are you standing, sitting, or lying down? Are you resting, relaxing, or doing something?

_____

_____

_____

_____

Imagine and describe how your body and spirit feel in this place.

_____

_____

step 2

Describe an event in the past when you did something you were afraid to do, and the result turned out to be mostly positive.

_____
_____
_____

What did you learn from this experience of facing your fear and pushing through it?

_____
_____
_____

step 3

Describe an upcoming event or situation that is causing you to feel fear. It may or may not be a totally scary or daunting event, but one that is causing you to have serious concerns or doubts for one reason or another.

_____
_____
_____
_____

step 4

Circle 2-3 of the following words that apply to the event or situation you described in step 3.

agitation	apprehension	distress	jitters	worry	concern	intense discomfort
tension	self-doubt	dread	terror	fright	uncertainty	impending disaster
tightness	insecurity	urgency	alarm	panic	foreboding	helplessness
suspicion	anxiety	horror	danger	angst	fretfulness	hopelessness

step 5
Answer any of the following questions that apply to the fear you described in step 3.

How long have you felt this fear? _____

Has this fear served to protect you in any way? If so, how?

_____

_____

Is this fear serving you in any way now? If so, how?

_____

_____

Does this fear prevent you from doing things you want or need to do? If so, what?

_____

_____

step 6
Practice self-compassion by following these steps.

1. I acknowledge how stressful it is to feel this fear.
2. I give myself a kind thought and/or gesture, such as massaging my shoulders, holding my head, or taking a deep breath.
3. I know other people in the world are fearful for similar reasons; I'm not alone.
4. In my mind, I send compassionate thoughts to those people, far and near.

step 7
Select one of the provided wall photos from the following pages that best represents your wall of fear as it relates to the event or situation you described in step 3. Notice that the wall photographs are turned sideways on the workbook pages.

If you want to use a provided image more than once, photocopy it.

What is significant about the wall photo you selected?

_____

_____

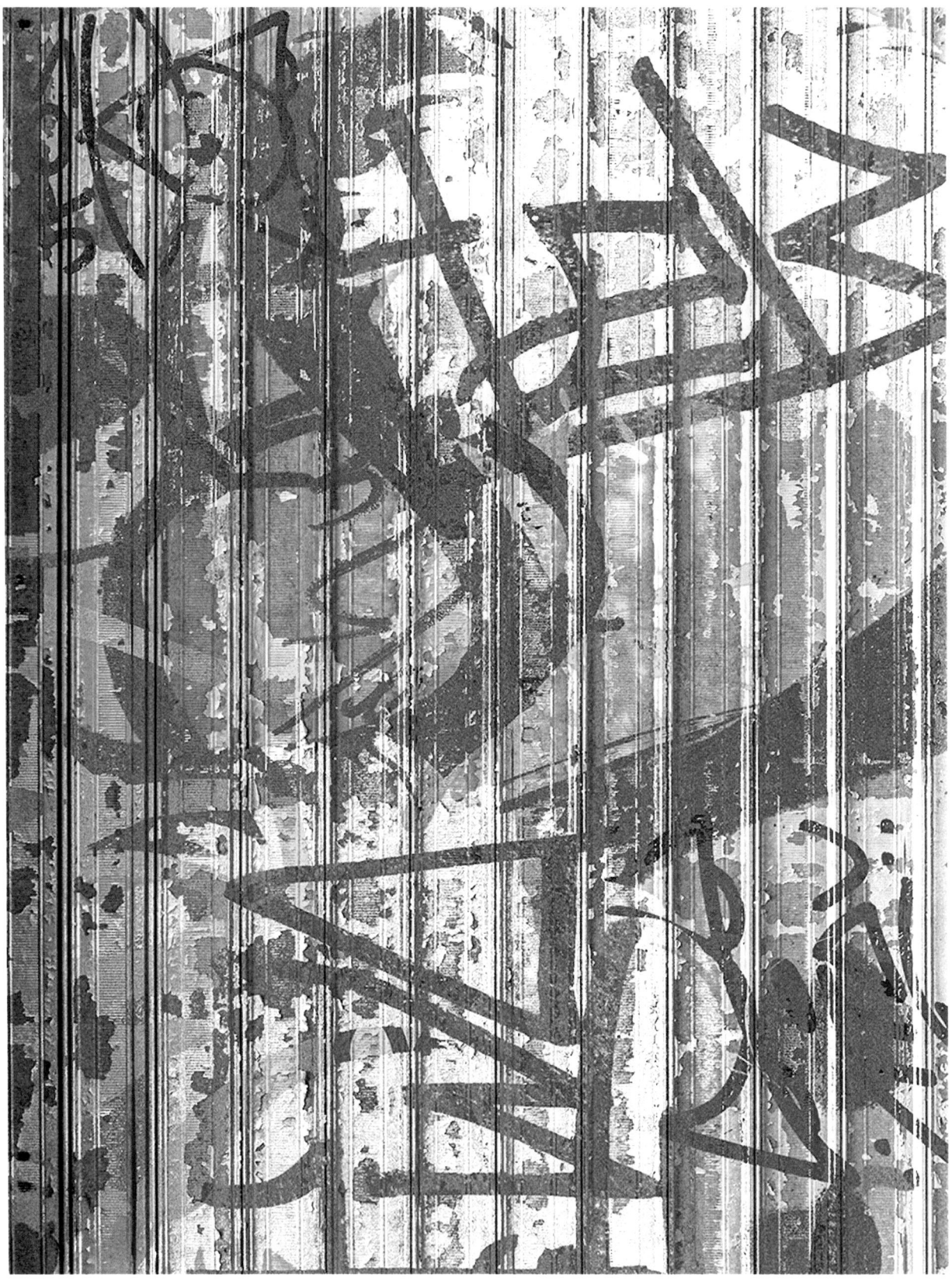

step 8
View the artwork examples at the beginning of this project for a visual reference as you follow the artmaking steps.

Trim off the white border around the outside edges of the wall image. With a pencil or pen, draw an outline of a door starting at the bottom of the wall image. Cut upwards along one side of the door and across the top of the door, so you can fold it back to open and close it.

step 9
Look through image sources (listed in the *PREPARATIONS* section) for an abstract, semi-abstract, or realistic image to represent something positive that could be waiting for you once you walk through the door. This image may contain colors, shapes, lines, people, animals, indoor or outdoor scenes, natural or man-made objects, art reproductions, or other visual elements.

Make sure the image you choose is at least a little larger than the door opening. To know how different images will look before selecting one, place your open-door wall over various pictures to see the effect.

step 10
Glue or tape the image to the back of the wall, being careful not to glue it to the door. Then glue the wall to a sheet of white mixed media paper without gluing the door, so you can still open and close the door.

Look closely at this image through the door. Describe the image you selected.

_____

_____

_____

_____

What meaning does this image hold for you?

_____

_____

_____

What are 1-3 real-life possibilities, opportunities, or achievements that might occur if you walk through the wall of your fear?

_____

_____

_____

step 11

Circle 1-3 strengths that will be most helpful to you as you face the wall and walk through the door.

courage	imagination	open-mindedness	hope	honesty	friendliness	practicality	determination
wisdom	resilience	self-acceptance	faith	integrity	enthusiasm	efficiency	willpower
intuition	endurance	self-regulation	grace	fairness	playfulness	competency	forgiveness
curiosity	adaptability	receiving support	humor	kindness	intelligence	productivity	gratitude
learning	willingness	giving support	energy	devotion	optimism	teamwork	mindfulness
creativity	flexibility	problem-solving	love	patience	spirituality	leadership	humility

Choose a different solid-color paper to represent each strength you circled. Write the names of colors you selected near the corresponding strengths you circled above, so you'll know which color represents which strength.

Cut out simple abstract or symbolic shapes from the solid-color papers to add to your artwork. Consider shapes that might represent a mantel over the door, a doorknob, doorframe, or windows. Or you may wish to cut out other symbolic shapes that can be placed anywhere on your artwork.

Glue these shapes to your artwork.

step 12

Are there supportive individuals or groups that might be helpful to you as you walk through the door? These may be people you already know or people you'll contact for the first time.

_____

_____

_____

Choose a different solid-color paper to represent these supportive people. Cut out a shape to represent supportive people. What color and shape represents your supports?

_____

Glue this shape to your artwork.

step 13

Look at your artwork from arm's length. Give it a title.

_____

step 14

In this step you'll be writing instructions or composing an instruction poem for how to walk through a wall of fear. Following are two examples of writing from artmakers who previously completed this project.

Instructions on How to Walk through a Wall of Fear

Surround yourself with spacious awareness; its endless energy is available to you. Stay calm. Walk up to the wall. Run your hands over the rough cement. Even though you're panicky, touch the smooth doorknob. Turn it. Peek inside. Smell the fresh lemon scent on the air. Step back. Know you can choose resilience no matter the outcome. Step up to your determination inviting you to enter. Take the next step over the threshold. Do not be deterred by doubt or disturbing forces. Walk through. Keep walking. A warm breeze softens your way.

Instructions on How to Walk through a Wall of Fear

Take a winding walk on the beach. Empty your mind of fear and doubt. Fill up with beauty and sounds of the ocean. Open up to confidence, faith, and hope.

Walk back toward the graffiti-filled wall. Deep breathe. Touch the doorknob. Feel the love for self. Use all your strength. Ask your loved ones for help. When you are ready, pull, believe, pull, trust, pull, hope.

Step into the sand and look at the open sky framed with a rainbow. Reach for the bird in flight over the waves. Listen for the guidance within you and spoken from the sky. Remember YOU are the only YOU.

You might begin your writing with the title: *"Instructions on How to Walk through a Wall of Fear."* If it's helpful, start with a description of your safe place: *"Stand still. Imagine a place that brings you calm and strength. Notice . . . "*

Look at your artwork and review your writing in this project. Describe how to approach the wall and what it looks like. Describe how to step up to the door. Include emotional, mental, and physical sensations.

Mention strengths and supports from steps 11 and 12. Describe how to open the door and step over the threshold. Describe what it might be like to walk into the new surroundings on the other side of the wall. Feel free to use any of the following phrases if they can be useful in your writing.

be aware of . . .	slowly . . .	survey the situation	gather your . . .
look around	listen for . . .	ponder the risks	put one foot in front of the other
move forward	with caution	touch the . . .	take another step
remember to . . .	one step	you can do this	stand on the threshold
when it's time	see the . . .	look up at the . . .	don't hesitate too long before . . .
steady your feet	go for it	when you're ready	take a deep breath
go slow	thinking	reach out	even though you're feeling . . .
why not now	now or never	ready set go	pass through the portal

Write the instructions or compose an instructional poem below that describes how to walk through your wall of fear.

Read your writing out loud so you can both see and hear it.

LIFE APPLICATIONS

- When facing this fear, ask yourself the following questions: In real life, is it reasonably safe for me to proceed? Do I need to ask the opinion of a trustworthy person as to how I should proceed?

- If you don't open the door and step through, what stressful problems or regrets will likely remain or occur?

- In most cases, your worst fear won't come true, but if it did, how would you cope in a healthy way?

Once you have a coping plan, you may feel a degree of stress relief as it will allow you to let go of the worry associated with a worst-case scenario.

- What is the first small, real-life step to take toward dealing with this fear?

CONCLUSIONS

- Note any useful insights, revelations, beliefs, or intentions that emerged while you worked on this project or that come to mind now.

- Detect any tension you're holding in your neck, shoulders, or elsewhere in your body. Consciously relax, pat, massage, or gently stretch those areas.
- If it's comfortable to do so, close your eyes and consciously enjoy three breaths.
- Notice where your body is contacting the chair, floor, or table. Look around the room. Experience a sense of being present in your body and surroundings as you finish.
- Sign and date your artwork. Store it for safekeeping.

project 18

UPDATE AN INTERPERSONAL LANDSCAPE

respect & validation

It's common to experience stress in relationships with other people, sometimes more so with those closest to us. Even if a relationship is basically supportive and positive, it can still be upsetting at times. We may be disturbed and disappointed with the behavior of another person and troubled by our own thoughts, actions, or words.

Since almost all of us want to be respected, understood, and validated for who we are, we can aspire to relationships that are based on acceptance and kindness. There's an art to respecting and validating the unique personality and viewpoint of another person while honoring our own needs, wants, and opinions.

We can recognize our diversity, differences, and separateness while exploring ways to connect and act with cooperation. We can move toward mutually supporting each other while doing what each of us wants to do as long as it doesn't negatively affect the other person. We can also learn how to be assertive without being aggressive, to calmly suggest or ask rather than make demands, to become collaborators instead of competitors, to speak without judgment, and to listen without fault-finding.

When we try to take the high road, sometimes the other person will join us. Whether or not that person can meet us there, we can still feel good about positive changes we make in ourselves.

It can be quite challenging to move forward in a relationship that has been largely difficult or destructive. There may be times when it's better to end a relationship rather than remain in one that's harmful. And there may be other times when we drift apart from someone due to life changes or lack of common interests or values.

To create a before-and-after makeover of a current relationship, you'll draw and combine two simple oil pastel landscapes. You'll also compose a mini story related to your artwork.

PREPARATIONS

- Clear and protect the surface of your artmaking table.
- Gather tools and materials: pen or pencil for writing
    8½"x11" or 9"x12" assorted solid-color papers
    scissors
    glue stick
    9"x12" white mixed media paper, 1 sheet
    oil pastels
    paper towel

- Minimize noise and the potential for interruptions.
- You may opt to work on this project in more than one sitting.
- If you experience a notable increase in your stress level while doing this project, take a break.
- As you follow directions, be curious and open to what occurs. Refrain from judging the correctness or quality of your artwork and writing.
- If it's comfortable to do so, close your eyes and consciously enjoy three breaths, being aware of the air moving through your nose or the expansion and contraction of your diaphragm.
- Notice where your body is contacting the chair, floor, or table. Look around the room. Experience a sense of being present in your body and surroundings as you begin.

DIRECTIONS

step 1

Most interpersonal relationships can use some improvement from time to time. Identify one relationship with a spouse, partner, family member, friend, co-worker, or another person that you're willing to explore in this project.

_____

What is one thing you value about this relationship?

_____

_____

What is one thing you value about the other person?

_____

_____

step 2

A biome is a geographic area with distinctive plants and animals that are sustained by that region's climate. Read through the list of biomes below. Circle one type of biome and any of its subcategories that metaphorically represents the current state of the relationship you identified in step 1.

FRESHWATER AQUATIC: spring   pond   lake   stream   creek   river   waterfall   bayou   marsh   bog   swamp   rapids   mud flat   fountain   floodplain

SALTWATER AQUATIC: coral reef   beach   lagoon   deep-sea   seabed   tide pool

DESERT: wide-open   hot and dry   sand dunes   semi-arid   cold   coastal   high elevation   low elevation   dustbowl   badlands   wasteland   arid

FOREST: deciduous   woodland   pine   backwoods   grove   timberland   orchard

JUNGLE: tropical   wilderness   rain forest   dense   tangled

SHRUBLAND: scrub   brush   chaparral   heath   moor   range   outback   thicket   bramble

GRASSLAND: savanna   grassy plain   prairie   meadow   pasture

TUNDRA: arctic   polar   alpine   mountain   plateau   flatland   icy

What is the atmosphere, weather, and climate like? Are there seasonal changes? Are there storms of any kind? What plant material is in this biome?

_____

_____

What do you like about this biome? _____

_____

What do you dislike about this biome? _____

_____

step 3

Choose a solid-color sheet of paper for the background of this biome. Cut it in half. On one half-sheet, use the ends and/or sides of oil pastels to depict this biome abstractly or semi-realistically with colors, lines, shapes, and forms. If you want, you can use a small piece of clean paper towel to blend or smooth colors.

Describe this artwork.

_____

_____

step 4
If you were an animal, bird, reptile, insect, fish, or aquatic mammal in this biome, what would you be? What would the other person be?

step 5
If this relationship could be improved, which metaphoric biome and its subcategories listed in step 2 would best describe this improved relationship?

What is the atmosphere, weather, and climate like in this updated biome? Are there seasonal changes? Are there storms of any kind? What plant material is in this biome?

step 6
What is preferable about this biome as compared to the biome you identified in step 2?

step 7
Choose a solid-color sheet of paper for the background to represent this biome. Cut it in half. On one half-sheet, use the ends and/or sides of oil pastels to depict this biome abstractly or semi-realistically with colors, lines, shapes, and forms. If you want, you can use a small piece of clean paper towel to blend or smooth colors.

Describe this artwork.

step 8

If you were an animal, bird, reptile, insect, fish, or aquatic mammal in this preferred biome what would you be? What would the other person be?

step 9

Typically, there are transition zones between biomes that combine elements of each. These zones are called ecotones.

Combine elements of your two biome drawings to create an ecotone/transition zone. Feel free to cut, tear, weave, and/or overlap your drawings. Arrange your collage elements on white mixed media paper. Once you're satisfied with the arrangement, glue the elements to the white surface. If you want, add more oil pastel details.

Describe this new artwork.

step 10

In this step you'll be writing a mini story that describes the progression as both of you move from the initial biome through the ecotone/transition zone to a preferred biome. Following are two examples of writing from artmakers who have previously completed this project.

TWO WORLDS

Life in the arctic is barren, yet beautiful. The massive icebergs are made whiter by the surrounding Prussian blue water. The clear sky is dotted with clouds ready to release more heavy snow. A polar bear ambles around the snow looking for sustenance. A gentle harp seal swims in the water and shuffles on the ice with her pups, exploring and retreating. She steers away from the polar bear yet wants to move closer. Maybe this polar bear can protect or will it only hunt?

It felt like a miracle when an icy path appeared out of nowhere. It meandered towards a tree grove. Beautiful, lush woods framed by mountains with warm sunlight that glistens on the waving leaves. We change forms. He becomes a strong buck. I become a graceful doe. We marvel at the bounty of food: berries, seeds, leaves, and grass growing along a freshwater stream. We walk together on and off the paths. We look for a sheltered bed of leaves to call home. We curl up with our fawns and rest in our nest. Home at last.

WALKABOUT

The sky is overcast but it rarely rains. We amble through sagebrush and tumbleweeds like bobcats. Gnats circle and buzz around our eyes. We sniff grassy shoots emerging from the scattered rocks on the hard ground. We don't see anything green for the rest of the day. The next morning, we mutually decide to venture out again. This time we nibble on thin patches of grass here and there, sharing the fresh greens. The clouds lighten. We slowly walk toward some bright, red-colored shapes in the distance. Will they turn out to be cardinals or flowers?

Write your mini story on the blank lines below. You may want to include answers to some of the following questions in your writing.

> Are you walking, running, crawling, ambling, staggering, shuffling, limping, marching, dancing, faltering, swimming, drowning, paddling, floating, flowing, lurching, spinning, reeling, skipping, flying, soaring, and/or wandering?
>
> What plants, weeds, flowers, bushes, trees, or other things do you see? What do you hear and smell? What does the sky look like? Is the ground dry, wet, sandy, graveled, rocky, dusty, soft, hard? What is the weather like?
>
> What changes do you experience as you move through the transition area between biomes? Do the two of you stay together, explore different directions at times, go your separate ways, or make a fresh start?

_____
(title)

_____
_____
_____
_____
_____
_____
_____
_____

Read your story out loud so you can both hear and see the words.

What do some of the biome elements in your story represent in your real-life relationship?

_____
_____

step 11
Look at your artwork. Give your artwork and writing a title.

_____

LIFE APPLICATIONS

- On a separate sheet of paper, answer the following questions.

  In what positive ways do you contribute to this relationship?
  In what positive ways does the other person contribute to this relationship?

  What can you thank this person for that you ordinarily take for granted?

  What is one way you can feel compassion for this person instead of judgment?

  If you could change one thing about your thoughts, expectations, actions, and manner of speaking or acting in this relationship, what would it be?

  What is one way you could offer more respect, validation, or support to the other person while respecting your own individuality and the differences between the two of you?

  Consider whether a current conflict may be connected to something negative you experienced in the past. If you let go of this link, how can you see your relationship more clearly in the present?

  Even if you disagree, how can you listen deeply to the other person without criticism and without giving advice unless it's asked for?

  Are you willing to address conflicts instead of avoiding or minimizing them?

  Do you want to stay in this relationship, give it more time, fortify it, or move on?

- If you're experiencing a repetitive pattern of blaming one other, can you discuss this in a way so the other person can hear what you have to say? Below is one example of how to do this.

  When _____ happens (or doesn't happen), I feel _____
  because _____. The more I _____, the more you _____.
  There's no need to blame either one of us. We're both stuck in this pattern of reaction.

CONCLUSIONS

- Note any useful insights, revelations, beliefs, or intentions that emerged while you worked on this project or that come to mind now.

  _____

  _____

- Detect any tension you're holding in your neck, shoulders, or elsewhere in your body. Consciously relax, pat, massage, or gently stretch those areas.
- If it's comfortable to do so, close your eyes and consciously enjoy three breaths.
- Notice where your body is contacting the chair, floor, or table. Look around the room. Experience a sense of being present in your body and surroundings as you finish.
- Sign and date your artwork. Store it for safekeeping.

project **19**

A WEAVING TO HELP WITHSTAND LOSS

consolation & endurance

Significant levels of stress may result from the loss of someone or something that has been meaningful to us. We experience many losses in our lives which may include the loss of loved ones, friends, pets, jobs, homes, financial security, precious irreplaceable objects, and previous levels of physical or mental wellbeing. We may even feel grief related to something we never had or experienced, such as the loss of a normal childhood, an unknown parent, or unfulfilled goals and opportunities. Following trauma, some people may experience the loss of their previous sense of safety, trust, and self-image.

Each one of us responds to loss in different ways at different times. We may experience immediate anguish, recurrent waves of emotion, a delayed reaction, or denial. Anger, guilt, and fear may accompany a loss as well as confusion and physical distress. It may take longer to accept sudden or inconceivable losses, especially those without a reasonable explanation or those that cause difficult life changes.

There is no standard rule or normal guideline for how we deal with loss. Even so, we can feel the emotions, honor what has been lost, and continue to engage in life to one degree or another. Over time, anguish and sorrow may become less intense.

In this project you'll create a paper weaving, using a found image to represent the aftereffects of your loss and paper strips to represent self-compassion. You'll identify self-care strategies, strengths, and supports that can help you work with the loss and any ensuing changes in your life. You may also choose to follow directions for a structured writing activity that addresses your loss.

PREPARATIONS

- Clear and protect the surface of your artmaking table.
- Gather tools and materials: pen or pencil for writing
  scissors
  glue stick
  9"x12" white mixed media paper, 1 sheet
  8½"x11" or 9"x12" assorted solid-color papers
  image sources, such as used magazines, books, newspapers, brochures, catalogs, old calendars, greeting cards, photocopies, online printouts, your own photos

- Minimize noise and the potential for interruptions.
- You may opt to work on this project in more than one sitting.
- If you experience a notable increase in your stress level while doing this project, take a break.
- As you follow directions, be curious and open to what occurs. Refrain from judging the correctness or quality of your artwork and writing.
- If it's comfortable to do so, close your eyes and consciously enjoy three breaths, being aware of the air moving through your nose or the expansion and contraction of your diaphragm.
- Notice where your body is contacting the chair, floor, or table. Look around the room. Experience a sense of being present in your body and surroundings as you begin.

DIRECTIONS

step 1
What are one or two healthy ways you have experienced comfort and support in your life?

step 2
Describe one significant loss that continues to affect you.

step 3
Circle 3-5 words that best describe your emotional and mental state as it relates to that loss.

miserable	fearful	shocked	lonely	numb	bitter
sorrowful	jealous	impulsive	regretful	resentful	conflicted
frustrated	guilty	panicked	disappointed	confused	mistrustful
threatened	impatient	grieved	insecure	uneasy	overwhelmed
empty	suspicious	anxious	heartbroken	despairing	muddled
dreading	envious	agitated	gloomy	cautious	doubtful
irritated	depressed	chaotic	apprehensive	humiliated	angry

Are you experiencing any fear associated with this loss? If so, what is this fear about?

_____

_____

step 4
Is this loss affecting your physical state-of-being? If so, how?

_____

_____

step 5
To depict your emotional/mental/physical state as it relates to the loss, find a rectangular or square image that is at least as large as a half-page. Look through image sources (listed in the *PREPARATIONS* section) for an abstract, semi-abstract, or realistic image that may contain colors, shapes, lines, people, animals, indoor or outdoor scenes, natural or man-made objects, art reproductions, or other visual elements.

Describe this image.

_____

_____

step 6
Leave a ½"-1" UNCUT section across the top of the image.

From the bottom of the image, cut vertical strips up to the uncut section at the top of the image. Cuts can be straight or wavy and of varying widths.

Center the image on a sheet of white mixed media paper and glue the uncut section to the paper.

step 7

Practice the following steps of self-compassion:

1. I acknowledge how difficult this loss is.
2. I offer myself a kind thought and soothing gesture.

Considering the loss you described in step 2, checkmark any of the following thoughts or gestures that offer support, understanding, or comfort.

EXAMPLES OF SELF-COMPASSIONATE THOUGHTS:

This loss is hard for me right now.
It's ok to give attention to myself.
I can get through this safely.
My strengths and values can help me.
I give gentle warmth and caring to myself.
I show up for myself no matter what.
I respect my feelings.
I am a supportive friend to myself.
I offer myself reassurance.
I offer encouragement to myself.

This loss may not be as bad as I think.
I can let go of unnecessary suffering.
This is how it is for now.
I remind myself that everything is impermanent.
Something positive may come out of this loss.
It's understandable why this affects me.
I can give myself a break.
I give myself permission to relax.
I offer concern and comfort to myself.
I allow myself to feel hope.

Offer a kind thought to yourself by writing it on the blank line below. It could be one of the thoughts above, a combination of thoughts, or a thought you create for yourself now.

_____

EXAMPLES OF SELF-COMPASSIONATE GESTURES:

Massage my face and jaw.
Pat my head.
Soothe my forehead.
Take a short walk outside or inside.
Drink a glass of water or cup of tea.
Take a soothing bath or shower.
Exercise.
Make a bowl of soup.
Eat a healthy snack.
Feel the outside air or breeze on my face.
Take a rest or a nap.
Give myself flowers.

Hold my hand over my heart.
Gently massage my stomach.
Hug myself.
Hold my own hand.
Take a conscious breath.
Read an inspirational passage.
Tap my shoulders with my fingertips.
Listen to comforting music.
Look up at the sky.
Watch the sunrise or sunset.
Go to a quiet place.
Cross my arms over my chest.

What is one of the above gestures or a different soothing gesture you can initiate now or after you finish this project?

_____

3. I know other people in the world are experiencing a similar type of loss; I'm not alone.
4. In my mind, I send compassionate thoughts to those people, far and near.

step 8

Select a solid-color sheet of paper to represent self-compassion. Is there anything significant about this color?

Cut this sheet into relatively straight ½"- 2" wide strips.

View the artwork examples at the beginning of this project to see some different types of weaving variations. You can weave strips in a simple over/under fashion or be freer with your weaving style. Your weaving can be tight or loose. You may want to weave around important details in the image so they can still be seen. You can weave strips straight across or at an angle.

When you finish your weaving, you may want to trim the ends of the solid-color strips or allow them to float past the edges of the image.

You'll need to glue the bottom edges of the vertical image strips to the white paper to keep the horizontal strips from falling out. You may also want to glue the ends of the horizontal strips on the sides of the weaving to keep them in place.

step 9

How will you know when your grief begins to lessen? Checkmark any of the following that apply:

I'll accept this loss.
Thoughts of this loss won't arise in my mind as often.
The intensity of sadness or anger will be less.
I'll engage in pleasant activities more often.
My sense of safety and security will increase.
My ability to concentrate on other things will increase.

I'll more quickly let go of thoughts about the loss.
The emptiness won't be so deep.
I won't be so worried.
I'll experience moments of happiness.
I'll appropriately trust other people.
I'll be less agitated.

step 10

In this step, you'll choose to write either three paragraphs or a three-stanza poem. Following are two examples of writing by artmakers who previously completed this project.

HOMELAND

Ground millions have stood on
Years and years and years.
Deep roots woven underneath
Feed four seasons of
So many majestic landscapes.

Lost Traditions
Lost Laws
Lost Service
Lost Honor
Lost Dignity
Lost Truth
Lost Love
Lost Unity
Lost Traditions

Allow for some hope.
Ask for comfort.
Fight for what was lost.
Hold your own heart.
Grab another's hand.
Reach out for faith.
Don't let go.

A DIFFERENT KIND OF WILDERNESS

I'm unable to be as I once was. What comes next? The view seems to be narrowing.

Before now, I could backpack to the top of a faraway mountain — such stamina and freedom. I could turn three hundred sixty degrees to see all I could see.

Yet, perhaps it is only now that I am more open sighted than ever before. Now I can go wildly in whatever imaginative direction I want. I can draw, paint, and write it!

Compose your writing on the blank lines below.

The first paragraph or stanza will express your emotions and thoughts related to your loss. You may want to include some of the words or phrases you wrote or circled in steps 2-5.

The second paragraph or stanza will acknowledge and honor what was lost.

The third paragraph or stanza will offer consolation and compassion. You may want to include some of the words or phrases you checkmarked or wrote in steps 7 and 9.

_____
(title)

_____
_____
_____
_____
_____
_____
_____
_____
_____

Read your writing out loud so you can both see and hear it. Title your writing and artwork.

LIFE APPLICATIONS

- When experiencing a deep loss, we often neglect our physical care. How can you better attend to your nutrition, hydration, sleep, exercise, or medical checkups?

- Are there individuals or groups that can provide support to you? If so, how will you connect with them?

- Read through this strengths list. Circle strengths that have or will help you deal with this loss.

courage	imagination	open-mindedness	hope	honesty	friendliness	practicality
wisdom	resilience	self-acceptance	faith	integrity	enthusiasm	efficiency
intuition	endurance	self-regulation	grace	fairness	playfulness	competency
curiosity	adaptability	receiving support	humor	kindness	intelligence	productivity
learning	willingness	giving support	energy	devotion	optimism	teamwork
creativity	flexibility	problem-solving	love	patience	spirituality	leadership
willpower	gratitude	determination	trust	humility	forgiveness	mindfulness

- Specifically, how will you use one of these strengths to continue dealing with your loss?

- Checkmark any of the following phrases that might be helpful to repeat to yourself when needed.

    I find the inner strength to feel the pain of this loss.
    I'm aware that loss is part of life.
    I can accept this loss knowing I am more than my suffering.
    I acknowledge the anger and fear that may accompany this loss.
    When I'm ready, I can begin to fill the emptiness of this loss with new meaning or purpose.
    I'm aware that compassion and wisdom may emerge from dealing with this loss.

CONCLUSIONS

- Note any useful insights, revelations, beliefs, or intentions that emerged while you worked on this project or that come to mind now.

- Detect any tension you're holding in your neck, shoulders, or elsewhere in your body. Consciously relax, pat, massage, or gently stretch those areas.
- If it's comfortable to do so, close your eyes and consciously enjoy three breaths.
- Notice where your body is contacting the chair, floor, or table. Look around the room. Experience a sense of being present in your body and surroundings as you finish.
- Sign and date your artwork. Store it for safekeeping.

project 20

BALANCE ROCKS TO LIVE YOUR VALUES

purpose & meaning

New roles, life stages, lifestyles, and circumstances often call for the need to update our values. Without attention to our values, we may live passive, unfulfilled lives because we don't know what truly matters to us or we don't know how to apply our values to our everyday lives.

People care about different things for different reasons. It's important for each one of us to know what we truly value to avoid living by what other people think we should value. With better clarity and the commitment to live in alignment with our own values, our lives become more meaningful; we trust ourselves to make better decisions; and our self-worth improves, thereby reducing our stress.

Living our values isn't about having more; it's about living wiser with what we have. It's about taking better care of our lives and making insightful choices in the present that may influence the future in positive ways. When we decide to live in a value-oriented way, it helps us to move forward in the right direction. It's never too early or too late to start living our values.

In this project, you'll consider what matters most to you at this point in your life by creating a two-dimensional paper cairn from provided rock photos. You'll also write a short values statement that will help you stay on track.

Rock cairns can be seen in many parts of the world. People assemble them by balancing stones on top of one other. Cairns can indicate the location of a trail, imperceptible dangers (such as sudden drop-offs or potential mudslides), and scenic points. In some cultures, cairns are seen as wise guides or guardians. In any case, cairns are reminders to be more aware of what is happening in the present and to make choices that align with our values.

PREPARATIONS

- Clear and protect the surface of your artmaking table.
- Gather tools and materials: pen or pencil for writing
    scissors
    glue stick
    9"x12" white mixed media paper, 1 sheet

- Minimize noise and the potential for interruptions.
- You may opt to work on this project in more than one sitting.
- If you experience a notable increase in your stress level while doing this project, take a break.
- As you follow directions, be curious and open to what occurs. Refrain from judging the correctness or quality of your artwork and writing.
- If it's comfortable to do so, close your eyes and consciously enjoy three breaths, being aware of the air moving through your nose or the expansion and contraction of your diaphragm.
- Notice where your body is contacting the chair, floor, or table. Look around the room. Experience a sense of being present in your body and surroundings as you begin.

DIRECTIONS

step 1

From the list below, circle 5-7 of your most important personal values. Ask yourself what things you're passionate about, what motivates you, what makes you feel alive, what drives you forward, what means the most to you in your life.

family	service	success	wisdom	balance	teamwork
friendship	peace	bravery	joy	integrity	knowledge
marriage	freedom	prestige	play	financial security	education
commitment	responsibility	career	humor	mental health	recreation
parenting	security	diversity	beauty	physical health	religion
pets	loyalty	generosity	honesty	physical fitness	spirituality
community	justice	love	trust	relaxation	authenticity
nature	creativity	faith	gratitude	meditation	adventure
safety	home	comfort	job	ethical behavior	equality

List important talents, skills, or interests you have developed that are valuable to you.

_____

_____

Is there a value you left behind that you would like to reclaim now? If so, what is it?

_____

step 2

Notice whether any of your values relate to other values. For instance, some people connect nature with recreation, whereas other people may connect nature with spirituality. Some people may link knowledge with wisdom or link knowledge with a job. Note any connections between your values below.

step 3

If you had only one more day to live, what would you want to do on that day?

What is something you do most every day that you would *not* want to do on your last day of being alive?

step 4

On the following page, you'll find a template for a cairn that will serve as a mock-up for assembling your rock-photo cairn in steps 6 and 7.

Write each of your most meaningful values from step 1 inside a stone shape, one value per stone. Consider which value you want as the foundation stone at the bottom of your cairn and which one you'd like at the top. If you need more stone shapes for additional values, draw them on the template.

step 5

Starting with the topmost rock of your template on the previous page, note the specific personal importance of each value to you.

step 6
To represent each of your most important values, cut out one of the provided rock photos on the following pages. You can photocopy the pages to preserve the images in the workbook if you want.

step 7
On a sheet of white mixed media paper, arrange your paper rocks to construct a cairn.

Glue the paper rocks to the surface when you're satisfied with the arrangement.

On the back of your artwork, you may want to identify the value represented by each rock.

step 8

Look at your artwork. Imagine it's as tall as you are. It's located on the trail of your life. In your imagination, walk around it, view it from all sides, touch it.

Imagine your cairn represents a wise guide or guardian who reminds you of the values you hold dear. What supportive suggestions or advice does this guide or guardian have for you about your current life and the direction of your path and journey forward?

What are you honestly most passionate about? What makes you feel good or pleasantly energized? What truly matters most to you right now? What does it all come down to?

step 9

In this step you'll be writing a short personal values statement that summarizes your core values. Following are two examples of statements written by artmakers who have previously completed this project.

I commit to living my daily life guided by love and the following values: honesty, service, equality, creativity, and simplicity.

With joyful effort, be conscious, curious, creative, compassionate. Take care of what I've got. Let go of unnecessary suffering. Celebrate being alive. Be kind.

In 25 words or less, write your statement on the blank lines below. A statement of this length is easier to read and remember. Your statement needs to be true to you, realistic, and livable. It won't be perfect, but you can refine and update it from time to time.

In preparation for writing your statement, you may want to review your notes in steps 1, 2, 3, 5, and 8.

_____
_____
_____
_____
_____
_____
_____
_____

Read your statement out loud. Keep it on hand or memorize it.

LIFE APPLICATIONS

- If possible, read or recite your values statement each day so you can use it as a guide to plan activities and live your life. Your thoughts, actions, and life won't always align with your values, but whenever you're making an important decision or determining a goal, you can ask yourself if it's in general agreement with your values statement.

- What is one decision you want or need to make in your life now or in the near future?

  Which values are involved in making this decision?

  What action (or non-action) best aligns with your values? How will you proceed?

- Is there one of your values that needs more attention now? If so, how, when, and where will you give time and energy to promote that value?

- Remind yourself that small thoughtful steps on your path generally lead to better outcomes.

- You can revisit your art and writing from this project if it will benefit your ongoing personal growth and quality of life. Your values will change with time. You may want to repeat this project occasionally to update or reinforce your values.

CONCLUSIONS

- Note any useful insights, revelations, beliefs, or intentions that emerged while you worked on this project or that come to mind now.

- Detect any tension you're holding in your neck, shoulders, or elsewhere in your body. Consciously relax, pat, massage, or gently stretch those areas.
- If it's comfortable to do so, close your eyes and consciously enjoy three breaths.
- Notice where your body is contacting the chair, floor, or table. Look around the room. Experience a sense of being present in your body and surroundings as you finish.
- Sign and date your artwork. Store it for safekeeping.

project 21

DECLARATIVE ART FOR COLLECTIVE TRAUMA

impact & empowerment

NOTE: To lessen the possibility of compounding negative stress, before engaging in collective trauma work, it's best to process any previous individual trauma you have experienced in a safe and supportive environment, preferably under the guidance of a knowledgeable counselor or therapist.

Collective trauma affects specific groups of people who have witnessed or experienced traumatic events or situations that have involved actual or threatened bodily injury or death. Causal examples resulting in collective trauma include—but are not limited to—genocide, war zone exposure, famine, natural and man-made disasters, epidemics, mass shootings, terrorism, and violence associated with oppression, racism, religious discrimination, cultural and political conflicts, and human rights violations.

Negative physical, psychological, behavioral, relational, economic, political, and spiritual effects may result from collective trauma. Under certain circumstances, effects of trauma may be passed down to descendants of survivors.

To begin recovery from collective trauma, we can acknowledge and accept what has happened or is continuing to happen along with the past and current impact. Connections or community gatherings with others who have experienced the same type of collective trauma can provide social support. Traditional or nontraditional healing activities, such as art, writing, music, dance, theatre, prayer, meditation, and ceremonies can promote compassion, empowerment, and resilience.

When human beings inflict trauma on groups of people, it's often denied, minimized, or allowed to continue to avoid responsibility or to profit from wrongdoings. Addressing collective guilt, whether the harm was willingly or unintentionally caused, and seeking ways to provide amends and justice can be helpful to lessen anguish on all sides.

Many questions arise when we consider the field of collective trauma. How do we learn to be more humane? Can we work toward alternative narratives that honor diversity? Can we safeguard the survival of our species and planet? How will we be able to evolve our collective awareness into a higher state of consciousness? In this project you'll use oil pastels and writing to explore and express your responses to collective trauma.

PREPARATIONS

- Clear and protect the surface of your artmaking table.
- Gather tools and materials: pen or pencil for writing
  black chisel-tip marker
  scissors
  glue stick
  9"x12" tracing paper, 1 half-sheet
  oil pastels
  9"x12" white mixed media paper, 1 sheet
  paper towel

- Minimize noise and the potential for interruptions.
- You may opt to work on this project in more than one sitting.
- If you experience a notable increase in your stress level while doing this project, take a break.
- As you follow directions, be curious and open to what occurs. Refrain from judging the correctness or quality of your artwork and writing.
- If it's comfortable to do so, close your eyes and consciously enjoy three breaths, being aware of the air moving through your nose or the expansion and contraction of your diaphragm.
- Notice where your body is contacting the chair, floor, or table. Look around the room. Experience a sense of being present in your body and surroundings as you begin.

DIRECTIONS

step 1
Do you belong to any specific groups of people that have been affected by serious discrimination, prejudice, maltreatment, stereotyping, harassment, bullying, brutality, injustice, inequality, devaluation, genocide, or hostility that have led to threats or actual injury or death due to group identity? If so, what groups?

___

___

step 2
List any other specific groups you directly identify with that have been seriously threatened by war, epidemics, man-made or natural disasters, or other traumatic circumstances.

___

___

step 3

Have any of your ancestors or close relatives experienced collective trauma by belonging to a specific group of people? If so, what group and how were they affected? How have you been affected by their trauma?

_____

_____

_____

step 4

Circle 3-5 words that best describe the negative impact on groups of people you identified in steps 1-3.

shock	desperation	helplessness	alarm	anger
agitation	job loss	hopelessness	panic	rage
instability	social isolation	harassment	anxiety	hate
conflict	property damage	invalidation	terror	poverty
exasperation	hypervigilance	invisibility	horror	aggravation
uncertainty	suspicion	injury	fear	frustration
mistrust	disconnection	illness	death	sorrow
uneasiness	tribulation	victimization	threat	grief
worry	demoralization	weariness	dread	injustice
concern	physical impairment	exhaustion	disgust	oppression
confusion	vulnerability	cynicism	anguish	humiliation
resentment	dejection	numbness	shame	devaluation

step 5

Select a different oil pastel color to express each word you circled in step 4. Put a dab of each color next to the corresponding word.

On a half-sheet of tracing paper, create an abstract artwork using straight, curved, diagonal, choppy, and scribbled lines, cross hatching (closely spaced intersecting parallel and perpendicular lines), or simple shapes. Use all or some of the colors you selected in the previous steps. You may want to blend or smear colors with a small clean piece of paper towel. Set your artwork aside for now.

step 6

Take a moment to practice compassion.

1. I acknowledge the impact of collective stress or trauma on myself.
2. I offer a kind thought or gesture to myself, such as giving myself some flowers, touching my shoulder, or holding my head with both hands.
3. I know others in the world are experiencing this type of collective stress; I'm not alone.
4. In my mind, I send compassionate thoughts to those people affected by collective trauma.

step 7

In this step you'll be composing three short declarations that carry your expressive voice for empowerment and an improved collective future for any groups you identified in steps 1-3. You might view these declarations as messages on posters, protest signs, or shields against collective trauma.

Examples of writing from artmakers who previously completed this project are below.

LEARN TO BE HUMAN	SPEAK PEACE	BE KIND
SURVIVAL FOR ALL	RECLAIM JUSTICE	EQUALITY
RESUSCITATE OUR PLANET	SEARCH FOR TRUTH	MAKE IT REAL AGAIN
RESIST INSIST PERSIST	RIGHTS ARE RIGHTS	DO THE RIGHT THING
PROTECT OUR CHILDREN	HONOR DIVERSITY	CHOOSE LOVE

For inspiration, you can fill in the blanks below with any of the words or phrases that follow.

say yes to _____	foster _____	enhance _____	cherish _____
aspire to _____	nurture _____	promote _____	reclaim _____
reinvent _____	search for _____	rise to _____	protect _____
humanitarian efforts	responsible actions	understanding	empowerment
interconnection	being alive on earth	global unity	reparation
peacemaking	goodwill to all	real change	wellbeing
shared happiness	humane evolution	truth	safety
our collective worth	the will to heal	compassion	health
equality	ethnic diversity	civility	reconciliation
healing	support systems	preservation	cohesion
trust	equal rights	survival	transparency
cooperation	sustainable future	mindful action	respect
vindication	endurance	group camaraderie	empowerment
kindness	goodness	human rights	good faith
hope	charity	benevolence	decency
honesty	justice	help	fairness

Write 1-3 short declarations below.

_____

_____

_____

step 8

Apply glue on the *frontside* corners of your artwork. Turn your artwork *face down* in the center of a sheet of white paper. Secure the corners.

Imagine your artwork is the size of a poster or sign. Using a chisel-tip marker, print one of the declarations you wrote in step 7 on the artwork you have glued down.

Read your declaration out loud with a strong voice of conviction.

step 9

Circle 1-3 strengths you most need to transform the stress associated with words you circled in step 4.

courage	imagination	open-mindedness	hope	honesty	friendliness	practicality	determination
wisdom	resilience	self-acceptance	faith	integrity	enthusiasm	efficiency	willpower
intuition	endurance	self-regulation	grace	fairness	playfulness	competency	forgiveness
curiosity	adaptability	receiving support	humor	kindness	intelligence	productivity	gratitude
learning	willingness	giving support	energy	devotion	optimism	teamwork	mindfulness
creativity	flexibility	problem-solving	love	patience	spirituality	leadership	humility

step 10

Checkmark or underline any of the following wellbeing strategies that will help you tolerate, lessen, or transform the responses to collective trauma you identified in step 4. (See Appendix A, page 260 for a detailed description of these wellbeing practices.)

PHYSICAL SELF-CARE: Attend to your nutrition and hydration, exercise, sleep routine, and physical and dental checkups. Follow through with recommendations from health providers.

SELF CHECK-IN: Identify your current emotions. Determine your state of mind. Do a quick body scan. Are you relatively ok in the present moment? If not, what do you need to attend to?

PAUSE / GO SLOWER: Take one or more conscious breaths. Be aware of inhaling and exhaling. Relax tense muscles.

PRESENT MOMENT AWARENESS: Be in the present moment, whether it's pleasant, neutral, or unpleasant. Be aware of what you see, hear, smell, taste, and touch. Acknowledge your thoughts and feelings. Allow them to pass through your mind and body without pushing them away or clinging to them.

COMPASSION: Acknowledge a problem or difficulty. Give a caring, kind thought and/or gesture to yourself. Know other people in the world are experiencing something similar; you're not alone. In your mind, send compassionate thoughts to those people, far and near.

MULTI-PERSPECTIVES: Look at any given situation from more than one point of view. See the bigger picture.

GRATITUDE: Take time to appreciate what is good in your life. Take care of your life. Take care of what you value in your life.

POSITIVE EXPERIENCES: Be aware of positive experiences while they're happening. Create more enjoyable moments in your everyday life.

SELF-ACCEPTANCE / SELF-VALIDATION: Accept your vulnerabilities, imperfections, talents, skills, and strengths without comparing yourself to others.

SOCIAL CONNECTIONS / SUPPORTS: If possible, connect with another human being in some way each day.

VALUES: Circle a few values below that are most meaningful to you. Live by them each day.

family	service	success	wisdom	balance	teamwork
friendship	peace	financial security	joy	integrity	knowledge
marriage	freedom	prestige	play	bravery	education
commitment	responsibility	career	humor	mental health	recreation
parenting	security	diversity	beauty	physical health	religion
pets	loyalty	generosity	honesty	physical fitness	spirituality
community	justice	love	trust	relaxation	authenticity
nature	creativity	faith	gratitude	meditation	adventure
safety	home	comfort	job	ethical behavior	equality

MEDITATIVE FOCUS / CONTEMPLATION: If possible, engage in meditation, yoga, tai chi, qigong, prayer, spiritual study, or another inspirational or contemplative practice each day.

DAILY RECAP: Review a difficult moment. Determine what made it difficult. What can you learn from this? What small choice did you make today to reduce your stress or create a positive experience. What are you most grateful for today?

How, when, and where will you activate 1-2 of the checkmarked wellbeing practices? Be specific.

_____
_____
_____
_____
_____
_____
_____
_____
_____

LIFE APPLICATIONS

- Would it be helpful for you to connect with other people who have experienced the same type of collective stress or trauma you have experienced? If so, how will you contact them?

- How can you use expressive methods, such as art, writing, music, dance, or ceremony to promote compassion, empowerment, and resilience as they relate to your collective trauma?

- As of now, have you observed any degree of repair, justice, or positive change that has occurred following your experience with collective trauma?

- What is one small choice or one way you can offer kindness to help create a better world? When, where, and how will you activate this choice or kindness?

- Using your imagination, what would a world with less collective stress be like?

- As human beings, almost all of us have been conditioned to discriminate against certain types and groups of people. Think deeply about your negative assumptions, feelings, and prejudices regarding certain groups or categories of people. How can you begin to revisit and revise your opinions in a positive way?

CONCLUSIONS

- Note any useful insights, revelations, beliefs, or intentions that emerged while you worked on this project or that come to mind now.

- Detect any tension you're holding in your neck, shoulders, or elsewhere in your body. Consciously relax, pat, massage, or gently stretch those areas.
- If it's comfortable to do so, close your eyes and consciously enjoy three breaths.
- Notice where your body is contacting the chair, floor, or table. Look around the room. Experience a sense of being present in your body and surroundings as you finish.
- Sign and date your artwork. Store it for safekeeping.

project **22**

COUNTERIMAGE YOUR WORLDVIEW

suffering & wonderment

In times of heightened personal or collective stress, crisis, or trauma, the world may seem unreliable, chaotic, and quite dangerous. This is compounded by news reports from around the world that are mostly negative, often tragic, and fear-inducing. Because of this, we may perceive the world through dark, smudged, and scratched lenses, barely able to see with any degree of clarity.

And yet, we can make it an everyday practice to clean our lenses, allowing a more expansive worldview that encompasses both suffering and joy. Through awareness and acceptance of both, we can better protect ourselves, others, and the world while enjoying the many incredible and meaningful things that surround us.

To reduce the impact of worry, fear, and stress, we can give ourselves a daily dose of wonderment. Mental and emotional moments of amazement, reverence, inspiration, beauty, and connection are important to sustain a balanced worldview. We can train ourselves to notice the extraordinary in the ordinary details of our day-to-day experiences and be grateful for small things and accomplishments.

In this project you'll use two images along with alphabet letters (W, O, R, L, D) to construct a collage. You'll also compose an acrostic poem, in which the first letter of each line vertically spells out the word, *WORLD*. Your poem may integrate the poetic device of alliteration, which is the repetition of similar sounds at the beginning of words.

PREPARATIONS

- Clear and protect the surface of your artmaking table.
- Gather tools and materials: pen or pencil for writing
  scissors
  glue stick
  9"x12" white mixed media paper, 1-2 sheets
  round/circular object such as a bowl, saucer, or drinking glass
  image sources, such as used magazines, books, newspapers, brochures, catalogs, old calendars, greeting cards, photocopies, online printouts, your own photos

- Minimize noise and the potential for interruptions.
- You may opt to work on this project in more than one sitting.
- If you experience a notable increase in your stress level while doing this project, take a break.
- As you follow directions, be curious and open to what occurs. Refrain from judging the correctness or quality of your artwork and writing.
- If it's comfortable to do so, close your eyes and consciously enjoy three breaths, being aware of the air moving through your nose or the expansion and contraction of your diaphragm.
- Notice where your body is contacting the chair, floor, or table. Look around the room. Experience a sense of being present in your body and surroundings as you begin.

DIRECTIONS

step 1
Recall a recent or past instance or place when you felt a sense of something wonderful, incredible, or amazing. Look through image sources (listed above in the *PREPARATIONS* section) for an abstract, semi-abstract, or realistic image that captures the essence or feeling you had at that time. This image may contain colors, shapes, lines, people, animals, indoor or outdoor scenes, natural or man-made objects, art reproductions, or other visual elements.

Use a circular object, such as a bowl or cup, to draw a circle on the image. Cut it out. Describe it below.

_____

_____

step 2
Find an image that captures the essence or feeling you have when you're aware of suffering in the world. As above, draw a circle on the image with a circular object such as a bowl or cup. Cut it out. Describe it.

_____

_____

step 3
Cut out five alphabet letters from the following pages to spell the word, *WORLD*. You can cut out the same or different-size letters. Photocopy the pages if you want to preserve them for future use.

LDD iFF DD

step 4

View the artwork examples at the beginning of this project for a visual reference as you follow the artmaking steps.

Depending on the size of the round-shaped images and the letters you cut out and the amount of white space you want in your collage, you'll need either one or two sheets of white mixed media paper for the background. If you need two sheets, tape the white paper together, side-by-side, along the length of the seam.

You may cut or tear the images and letters or leave them as is. Experiment with placing them to the edges, centered, or scattered over the surface. You may want to overlap them or place them sideways or upside down.

Move all the elements around on the paper until you're satisfied with the arrangement. Glue them to the white background paper.

step 5

Look at the "wonderment" image you selected in step 1.
Circle 1-3 words from each of the W, O, R, L, and D groupings on the next page that relate to that image or to the idea of wonderment in the world.

Write the words you circled below:

W: _____

O: _____

R: _____

L: _____

D: _____

step 6

Look at the "suffering" image you cut out in step 2.
Underline 1-3 words from each of the W, O, R, L, and D groupings on the next page that relate to that image or to thoughts of suffering in the world.

Write the words you underlined below:

W: _____

O: _____

R: _____

L: _____

D: _____

W

woebegone wonky worthwhile writhing water wildflowers walkways wholeness wires whatever withhold willful willingness want waking waltz wonderland war wily warning way warmth watchful waste waves worn out wahoo weariness weeping weighty welcoming wellbeing wacky wrecked whistles welded whiz wildlife whittles whoops winning wind window whole wings winks wisdom what-nots waver worry wholehearted worthiness wounds wide wishes workaday wavy wheezing wallowing warps waste wayward waylay weathered wrestling whiplash winsome wistful whip-stitched whispers wide-awake wilderness woodlands wondrous whorls wide-angled willowy wizard whirlwind windfall watchtower walk warmhearted wellspring

O

one one-way option otherwise owl opening operate onward opinions orange orchid opportunity order oscillation origin ordinary ousting ought ornaments outset ovation outcomes onrush outright opera oppression opulence ooze okay obtain object oblique obscure obstruct occupy opaque overture oxygen outflow omen omit occur ointment ominous offer omnipresence ongoing octaves observation orientation orchard offering overlook oblivion original obvious odyssey offensive offset offshoots off-track opening ornate oracles open-heart opposition optimum optical orbit outdoor orchestra ocean outreaching oasis open-air open-eyed optimism opportune opulent outcry orchid overabundance outgrowth

R

racket radiation raffle ragged rails rising rake rally rampant random range ransom river rare rash race rattle rays rave raw rebel restoration retreat reality rose readiness reap red reason rebound reciprocity receptive resistance risk rethink repel recovery rabbit revelation reduction reflection refuse remainder remedy rollick ribbon reverence repair regenerate renounce resort respect relentless righteous ring reel rabid radius rapid rapture remote rock rubble resource renewal rhapsody resilience radical radar radioactive raids reforest rainsquall resentment rapid right-minded raptor rationing raveling ravishing reasonable reflux refresh relay relax refuge release rescue replenishment revival radiance rainbow realization redemption resplendent resolution repeal

L

lookout lost loss love less lace little lag lament labyrinth limit limitless lark lucid laminate lariat lance lavish link leather leaps later lasting languish leaning leaks laceration left lackluster level levity latent linger listening leaving longing longsuffering longsighted loom launch luck luckless liveliness lurching lush lurking lures levers luminous larger-than-life learning liberation loco locomotive luster lunatic locate lock lawless lilt livid ledge lurid ledgers litany lemon lightening leaf lovelorn lowdown lullaby legible lack life leave liaison lingo latex listless loop loophole limbo loll lick lopsided lifelong lollipop lake light lavender luminescence lighter than air lionhearted longevity lotus laughter lovely lively

D

delicacy discovery daughter dahlia daystar dolphin dewdrop doggie duck difference damage daily danger dance dart dangle dazzling daylight dream dread default defy defect defensive dire delectable dependence deviation descent delusion dithering doom delivery desperation detect destiny dredge drift drop dust dwell dusk drumbeat debris dappled decoy decoration dog daze deal debacle decadence deception doubt daunting delay diatribe dizzy devotion division dragons devastation dauntless dismay dawn dreary daisy delight deceleration decent double declaration defraud degree delicate delirious dicey denial denatured deplete daffodil delicious diamond divinity dove disease

step 7

In this step, you'll compose an acrostic poem.
Following are two examples of writing from artmakers who have previously completed this project.

Water washes over warnings.
Once an oasis, now ominous.
Radioactive reverence.
Look for love where it is lawless.
Divinity, please defy the doom.

Waver among desperations.
Open-up to obscure observations.
Relentless leanings wink into regeneration.
Let luminescent optics
Define my daily discoveries.

Write your acrostic poem on the blank lines below. Use all or some of the words you wrote in steps 5 and 6. Consider adding other words from the W, O, R, L, and D word groupings along with words of your own.

Play with the arrangement of your words. You may want to modify your selected words by adding *-ing, -ed, -s, -ly,* or *-y* to the end of the words. You may also want to change nouns to verbs or adjectives or change verbs and adjectives to nouns.

W: _____

O: _____

R: _____

L: _____

D: _____

To make revisions, write or type your poem on a separate sheet of paper. Read your poem out loud.

step 8

Often it may seem as if there is more suffering in the world than wonderment. To protect ourselves, our brains are hard-wired to dwell on the negative instead of the positive. We need to pay extra attention to the life-affirming aspects within our world.

What are possible sources of wonderment readily available to you? What are other sources of wonderment you can seek out? Consider the following categories and fill in any blanks with specifics that you can apply to your life.

Be in nature: _____

_____

Read or view inspirational material: _____

_____

Research subjects that amaze you: _____

_____

Listen to upbeat music, look at enlivening art, or watch uplifting movies: _____

_____

Practice your spiritual or religious beliefs: _____

_____

Connect to other people, children, or pets: _____

_____

Engage in a creative activity such as art, music, writing, cooking, building, or gardening:

_____

Other potential sources of wonderment available to you: _____

_____

_____

_____

Remember to observe both wonderment and suffering. We need to stay open to both for the sake of humanity. Know that our world is never just an either/or proposition. There are also a multitude of events, situations, activities, and things that provide us with milder, more middle of the road experiences. Be sure to notice them as well.

LIFE APPLICATIONS

- Be open to wonderment whenever and wherever it presents itself.

- Seek out and create moments of wonderment. Each day, have a plan to experience wonderment in some way. What is your plan today?

  _____

- Is wonderment hiding somewhere nearby? Can you find wonderment in your immediate surroundings right now? If so, what is the nature of that wonderment?

  _____

- Find the extraordinary in something ordinary. Describe an example of this that exists in your life.

  _____

- Take a walk in the world. What do you see, hear, touch, and smell that brings a sense of wonderment to you?

  _____

- To be reminded of wonderment, place an inspiring object, piece of art, or quote where you can readily see it.

- What is one choice you can make now to protect a source of joy, beauty, amazement, or wonderment in the world?

  _____

- You can revisit your art and writing from this project if their messages and insights can be of help to balance your worldview. Repeat this project whenever you like.

CONCLUSIONS

- Note any useful insights, revelations, beliefs, or intentions that emerged while you worked on this project or that come to mind now.

  _____

  _____

  _____

- Detect any tension you're holding in your neck, shoulders, or elsewhere in your body. Consciously relax, pat, massage, or gently stretch those areas.
- If it's comfortable to do so, close your eyes and consciously enjoy three breaths.
- Notice where your body is contacting the chair, floor, or table. Look around the room. Experience a sense of being present in your body and surroundings as you finish.
- Sign and date your artwork. Store it for safekeeping.

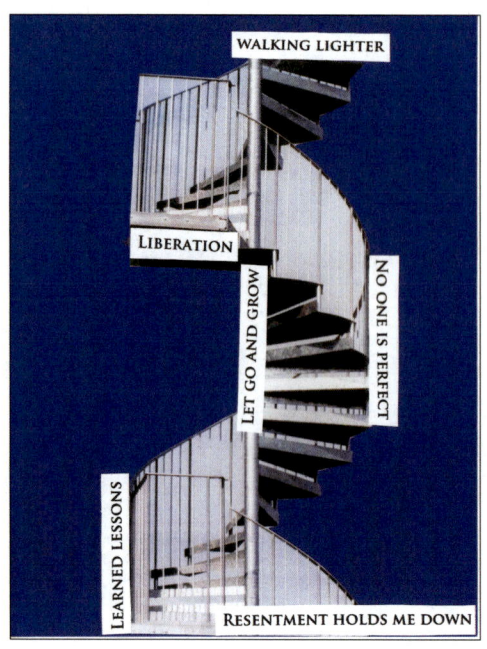
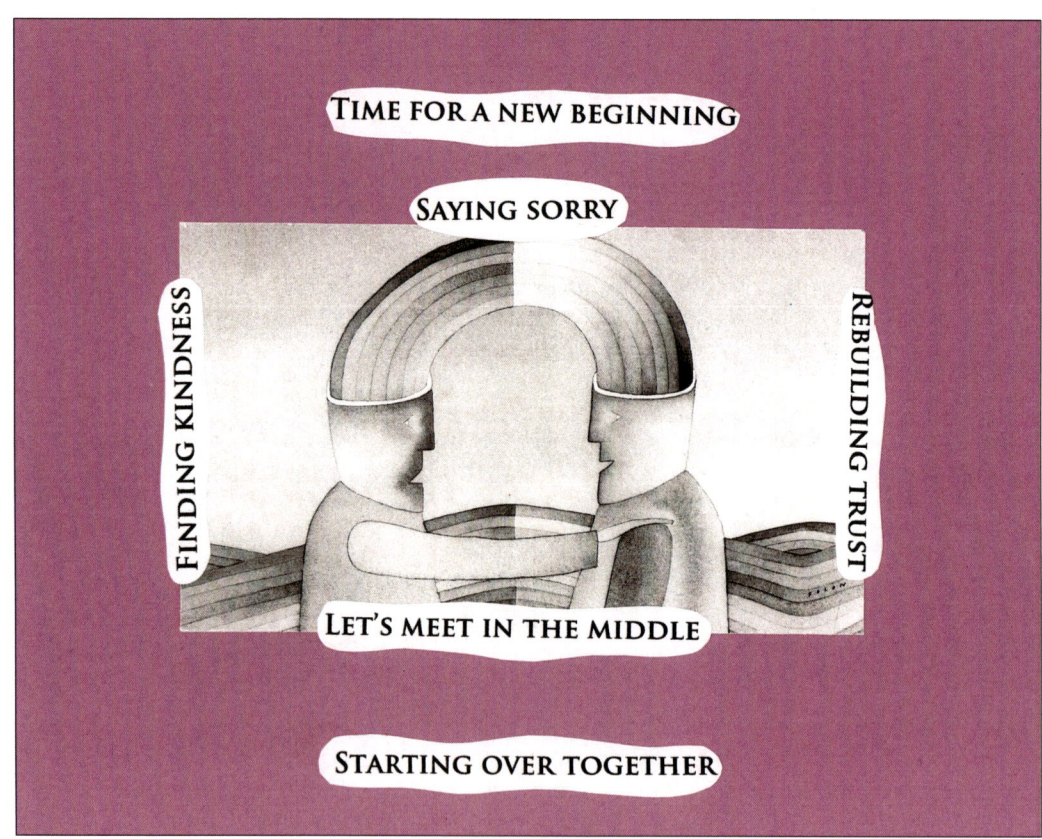

project **23**

VISIONS TO FORGIVE, RECONCILE, AND HEAL
release & recovery

Often when we've experienced stress, crisis, trauma, or been hurt in a relationship, we feel inclined to stay angry or hold resentments toward those involved. We may think it helps us to be angry, gives us power, punishes others, or shows that we're right. The important thing to consider when we hold onto these feelings and thoughts is that we may be hurting ourselves more than those who caused us pain. This can negatively impact our physical health, psychological wellbeing, and overall spirit. Three possible approaches to lessen anger and resentment within us are forgiveness, reconciliation, and healing.

Forgiveness is making the conscious choice to let go of hurt feelings, anger, grudges, or the need for vengeance toward others. It doesn't mean we forget, condone, or accept their offenses. Forgiveness can take place while we're still in a relationship or it may happen solely within us when those involved are no longer in our lives for one reason or another.

Reconciliation is making the choice to heal a relationship where hurt or pain has occurred. Both parties agree to express and process what happened, forgive one another, and continue to invest in the relationship's future. There is a mutual agreement to put the hurt or conflict in the past.

There are times we're unable or unwilling to forgive or reconcile when extreme abuse, hurt, or betrayal have occurred, especially when the other party hasn't acknowledged what happened, doesn't have remorse, continues to harm us physically or emotionally, or is no longer present. In these situations, it can be helpful and freeing to work toward inner healing. Healing involves doing the necessary personal work, so we're no longer held captive by pain, anger, fear, and resentment.

In this project, you'll use images, solid-color papers, and provided phrases to create three collages illustrating the concepts of forgiveness, reconciliation, and healing. You'll also compose a related piece of writing inspired by one of the phrases you chose.

PREPARATIONS

- Clear and protect the surface of your artmaking table.
- Gather tools and materials: pen or pencil for writing
  scissors
  glue stick
  8½"x11" or 9"x12" assorted solid-color paper
  image sources, such as used magazines, books, newspapers, brochures, catalogs, old calendars, greeting cards, photocopies, online printouts, your own photos
- Minimize noise and the potential for interruptions.
- You may opt to work on this project in more than one sitting.
- If you experience a notable increase in your stress level while doing this project, take a break.
- As you follow directions, be curious and open to what occurs. Refrain from judging the correctness or quality of your artwork and writing.
- If it's comfortable to do so, close your eyes and consciously enjoy three breaths, being aware of the air moving through your nose or the expansion and contraction of your diaphragm.
- Notice where your body is contacting the chair, floor, or table. Look around the room. Experience a sense of being present in your body and surroundings as you begin.

DIRECTIONS

step 1

Take a moment to reflect on the concept of forgiveness, remembering that forgiveness can occur with or without other people being an active part of the process.

Look through image sources (listed above in the *PREPARATIONS* section) for an abstract, semi-abstract, or realistic image to represent the concept of forgiveness. This image may contain colors, shapes, lines, people, animals, indoor or outdoor scenes, natural or man-made objects, art reproductions, or other visual elements.

You may find an image that works for you that is within a larger picture. For instance, it could be the image of a butterfly in surroundings that aren't right for your concept of forgiveness. You can simply cut out the butterfly and use just that part of the picture for your collage.

Make sure the final image is sized so it's smaller than a full sheet of solid-color paper.

step 2

Refer to the following pages of printed phrases. You can make copies of these pages if you want to use them again or want to have full use of all phrases printed on both sides of the pages. Cut out 1-6 phrases that relate to your understanding of forgiveness. Sometimes it works well to focus your mind on forgiveness while looking at the image you chose and picking phrases that jump out at you.

If you'd rather create and write your own phrases on your artwork, feel free to do so.

BREAKING DOWN BARRIERS	I AM SORRY
DO THE LOVING THING	HAVE MERCY
LOOK TO THE FUTURE	LETTING GO
HEALING THE WOUNDS	SAYING SORRY
GETTING ANOTHER CHANCE	I AM FREE
NURTURE MY BROKEN SELF	FREE YOURSELF
HEALING TAKES STRENGTH	LET IT GO
MY STORY MUST GO ON	LOVE, NOT FEAR
TRAPPED BY RESENTMENT	I AM HUMAN
HATE HAS NO HOME HERE	LIBERATION
TIME FOR A NEW BEGINNING	MOVING ON
LET'S MEET IN THE MIDDLE	TOGETHER
MAKING ROOM IN MY HEART	FREEDOM

TIME FOR A FRESH START	HEAL THYSELF
STARTING OVER TOGETHER	BREAK FREE
MAKING A FRESH START	YOU ARE FREE
NO LONGER HELD BACK	HOLDING MYSELF
MY SOUL NEEDS PEACE	I FORGIVE YOU
MENDING YOUR HEART	LOVE, NOT HATE
EVERYBODY HURTS	RELEASING ANGER
IT'S TIME TO MOVE ON	LET PEACE COME
MEND MY HEART	WALKING LIGHTER
MOVING FORWARD	LEARNED LESSONS
FINDING KINDNESS	ACCEPT APOLOGY
LOOKING FORWARD	SETTING ME FREE
LIVE, LEARN, LET GO	OPEN UP

PLEASE FORGIVE ME	YOU ARE HUMAN
SETTING YOU FREE	LET GO AND GROW
WE ARE ALL HUMAN	I DESERVE A FUTURE
HEALING TAKES TIME	I AM NOT PERFECT
LET THE LIGHT IN	HEALING WOUNDS
I DESERVE TO HEAL	REBUILDING TRUST
NO ONE IS PERFECT	SEEKING UNITY
TELLING THE TRUTH	SHARING MY HEART
YESTERDAY IS HISTORY	ON A NEW PATH
HOPE FOR TOMORROW	WE DESERVE PEACE
THE PAST IS IN THE PAST	I MISS YOU
REVIVE THE LOVE	LET IT BE
LESSONS ARE LADDERS	SEEING YOUR SIDE

PROTECT THE CONNECTION	BREATHE IN PEACE
RESTORE WELLBEING	REBOUNDING
BEFRIEND EACH OTHER	SOOTHE THE HURT
REVAMP AND REVISE	MAKE IT RIGHT
PATCH UP THE WOUNDS	REMEDIATION
WE BOTH DESERVE RESPECT	GET BETTER
CREATE THE HEALING	FIRST AID FIRST
STOP THE SUFFERING	REJUVENATION
ALLEVIATE THE HARM	EXTEND A HAND
REPAIR THE DAMAGE	GO TO BAT
MUTUAL RESOLUTION	UNDER MY WING
SETTLE INTO BETTER	BEGIN RECOVERY
SOOTHE AND IMPROVE	BENEFICIAL AID

step 3

Look through sheets of solid-color paper to choose a color that represents the feeling you might have after experiencing forgiveness. This will be the background for your image and printed phrases.

On this background, experiment with different arrangements of your forgiveness image and the printed phrases you cut out. You may place the words and phrases around your image, on top of your image, or elsewhere on the paper. Glue the elements down when you find an arrangement that is pleasing and makes sense to you. Write the word *forgiveness* on the back of this artwork.

As you look at your finished collage, is there a reason you arranged the elements as you did?

_____
_____
_____
_____

Are there any personal meanings associated with details in the image?

_____
_____
_____
_____

Is there an overall message or something more specific your artwork might be trying to tell you? There can be helpful messages if you look for them.

_____
_____
_____
_____

step 4

Take a moment to reflect on the concept of reconciliation, remembering that reconciliation occurs when you process a hurtful experience with someone in your life, choose to work together to forgive, and commit to continuing the relationship.

Look through image sources for an abstract, semi-abstract, or realistic image to represent the concept of reconciliation. This image may contain colors, shapes, lines, people, animals, indoor or outdoor scenes, natural or man-made objects, art reproductions, or other visual elements.

Cut out the image you chose in a way that works for you. Make sure the final image is sized so it's smaller than a full sheet of solid-color paper.

step 5

Refer again to the pages of printed phrases. Cut out 1-6 phrases that relate to your understanding of reconciliation. Sometimes it works well to focus your mind on reconciliation while looking at the image you chose and picking phrases that jump out at you.

step 6

Look through sheets of solid-color paper to choose a color that represents the feeling you might have after experiencing reconciliation.

On this solid-color paper, experiment with different placements of your reconciliation image and the printed phrases you cut out in step 5. You may place the words and phrases around your image, on top of your image, or elsewhere on the paper. Glue the elements down when you find an arrangement that is pleasing and makes sense to you. Write the word *reconciliation* on the back of this artwork.

As you look at your finished collage, is there a reason you arranged the elements as you did?

Are there any personal meanings associated with details in the image?

Is there an overall message or something more specific your artwork might be trying to tell you? There can be helpful messages if you look for them.

step 7

Take a moment to reflect on the concept of healing, remembering that healing can still occur even when you may not be able to forgive or reconcile with someone. Instead, you can choose to work through a painful or hurtful experience within yourself or in therapy to let go of the impact and move forward in your life with more freedom and peace.

Look through image sources for an abstract, semi-abstract, or realistic image to represent the concept of healing. This image may contain colors, shapes, lines, people, animals, indoor or outdoor scenes, natural or man-made objects, art reproductions, or other visual elements.

Cut out the image you chose in a way that works for you. Make sure the final image is sized so it's smaller than a full sheet of solid-color paper.

step 8

Refer once more to the pages of printed phrases. Cut out 1-6 phrases that relate to your understanding of healing. Sometimes it works well to focus your mind on healing while looking at the image you chose and picking phrases that jump out at you.

step 9

Look through sheets of solid-color paper to choose a color that represents the feeling you might have after experiencing healing.

On this background, experiment with different arrangements of your healing image and the printed phrases you cut out. You may place the words and phrases around your image, on top of your image, or elsewhere on the paper. Glue the elements down when you find an arrangement that is pleasing and makes sense to you. Write the word, *healing,* on the back of this artwork.

As you look at your finished collage, is there a reason you arranged the elements as you did?

_____
_____
_____
_____
_____

Are there any personal meanings associated with details in the image?

_____
_____
_____
_____
_____

Is there an overall message or something more specific your artwork might be trying to tell you? There can be helpful messages if you look for them.

step 10

In this step, you'll be creating a poem inspired by a phrase in one of your artworks. Following are two examples of writing from artmakers who previously completed this project.

SETTING ME FREE

The hands of love
Waited while I grew my wings.
The hands of peace
Cradled me while my wings dried.
The hands of freedom
Lifted me so I could take flight.

LIBERATION

Enough was enough.
Now it's time to climb.
Up and out from under.
One step then two then ten.
Hold the rail. Stop the railing.
No more sordid rumination.
Done with double dealing.
Spiral to the top. Fair skies.
Move up, move on.

Look at all three artworks. Read the phrases on your artworks out loud.

Choose one phrase that resonates the most with you now and write it on the first blank line below.

In response to that phrase, and while looking at the artwork that featured that phrase, write the first thing that comes to mind on the second line.

In response to the second line you wrote, write the first thing that comes to mind on the third line.

Don't try to plan or organize your thoughts, just let your written words on each line carry the next line forward in whatever way it happens to occur. Continue writing more lines until you sense you have written all that is needed.

_____

_____

_____

_____

_____

_____

_____

_____

_____

_____

_____

_____

_____

_____

_____

Read your writing out loud so you can both see and hear it. If you'd like, write, type, or revise your poem on a clean sheet of paper. Title your poem with the initial phrase that inspired your writing or with a different title that makes sense to you.

You can also write titles for each of your artworks. Write those titles on the back of your artworks.

Feel free to spend time now or later reflecting on your words and phrases. The total meaning of any artistic or creative endeavor may expand or change with additional contemplation.

You can do this writing exercise again with any of the other phrases you chose for your collages.

LIFE APPLICATIONS

- While working on these collages, you may have had thoughts or feelings related to a particular relationship or experience that has caused you pain or anger in the recent or distant past. Would you like to forgive or reconcile with this person, or would you like to work toward healing in some other way?

- Consider one small step you can take toward experiencing forgiveness, reconciliation, or healing. When, how, and where can you take this step?

  _____

  _____

- If you can release some of your anger, bitterness, resentment, hurt, and pain, what are one or two ways you may experience stress relief in your current life?

  _____

  _____

- Forgiveness, reconciliation, and healing related to severe stress or trauma can be challenging and distressing to work toward. It's recommended you seek support from a knowledgeable mental health, medical, or spiritual practitioner if you feel you need help to do this. Professional support can allow you to do this important work in a way that does not cause you to become overwhelmed or destabilized in your daily life.

- You can revisit your art and writing from this project if their messages and insights can be of benefit to you. Feel free to do this project more than once.

CONCLUSIONS

- Note any useful insights, revelations, beliefs, or intentions that emerged while you worked on this project or that come to mind now.

  _____

  _____

- Detect any tension you're holding in your neck, shoulders, or elsewhere in your body. Consciously relax, pat, massage, or gently stretch those areas.
- If it's comfortable to do so, close your eyes and consciously enjoy three breaths.
- Notice where your body is contacting the chair, floor, or table. Look around the room. Experience a sense of being present in your body and surroundings as you finish.
- Sign and date your artwork. Store it for safekeeping.

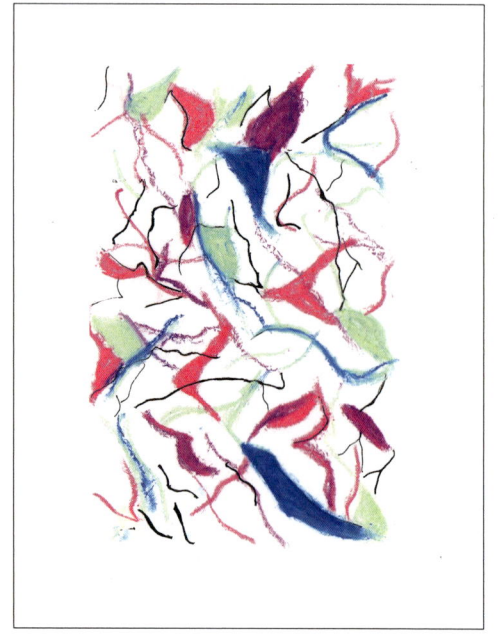

project 24

COLOR YOUR POST-TRAUMATIC GROWTH

adaptability & resiliency

Following severe stress, prolonged crisis, or traumatic events and situations, some people may become stronger, feel more alive, find increased enjoyment and meaning in their lives, and be better prepared to handle future adversities. This personal growth doesn't come automatically or quickly. It typically arrives with time and effort while continuing to manage the aftereffects along with other life challenges. Sometimes this growth can be so gradual, positive changes aren't readily apparent.

Trauma-related growth extends beyond basic coping and survival by embracing new and more valuable ways of being in the world. This growth comes in many forms. The specifics are unique to each person, but in general there are six categories in which people might achieve trauma-related growth:

- increased personal strengths
- enhanced wellbeing practices
- greater self-acceptance and self-worth
- improved interpersonal relationships
- amplified appreciation for being alive
- positive shifts in values and life priorities

You may not have experienced any growth so far, or you may have experienced growth in only one of the above categories. Without judgment, you can read through this project to become familiar with the potential for growth you may experience in the future.

Certainly no one would ever wish for someone to be exposed to severe stress in order to experience trauma-related growth. However, if someone has experienced a more extreme type of stress, why wouldn't that person strive for the growth that might result?

To explore personal growth possibilities, you'll create a mixed media artwork by crumpling a half sheet of tracing paper to represent the trauma, add markings to symbolize the aftereffects, and use oil pastels to color the growth you may have accomplished. You'll also complete a fill-in-the-blanks poem related to your artwork.

PREPARATIONS

- Clear and protect the surface of your artmaking table.
- Gather tools and materials: pencil and eraser
  black chisel-tip marker
  scissors
  glue stick
  9"x12" white mixed media paper, 1 sheet
  9"x12" tracing paper, 1 half-sheet
  oil pastels
  paper towel

- Minimize noise and the potential for interruptions.
- You may opt to work on this project in more than one sitting.
- If you experience a notable increase in your stress level while doing this project, take a break.
- As you follow directions, be curious and open to what occurs. Refrain from judging the correctness or quality of your artwork and writing.
- If it's comfortable to do so, close your eyes and consciously enjoy three breaths, being aware of the air moving through your nose or the subtle expansion and contraction of your diaphragm.
- Notice where your body is contacting the chair, floor, or table. Look around the room. Experience a sense of being present in your body and surroundings as you begin.

DIRECTIONS

step 1
Briefly note one event or situation of severe stress, prolonged crisis, or trauma you have endured in the past. This experience may have occurred over minutes, hours, days, weeks, or years. It may have taken place when you were a child, adolescent, or adult.

___

To represent this event or situation, crumple a half-sheet of tracing paper into a tight ball then slowly open your fist.

step 2
Practice the following steps of self-compassion, while gently holding the ball in both hands.

1. I acknowledge how difficult it was for me to experience this extreme stress, prolonged crisis, or trauma.
2. I give myself a kind thought and/or gesture, such as patting my arms, soothing my forehead, or placing my hand over my heart.
3. I know other people in the world have experienced similar severe stress, prolonged crisis, or trauma; I'm not alone.
4. In my mind, I send compassionate thoughts to those people, far and near.

Uncrumple the paper ball until it's relatively flat. It may have ripped in some places. Lay it on the table.

step 3

Identify any remaining aftereffects you're experiencing that relate to the severe stress, prolonged crisis, or trauma you noted in step 1. Examples of possible aftereffects may include—but are not limited to—physical problems, anxiety, depression, hopelessness, helplessness, insomnia, numbness, confusion, exhaustion, hypervigilance, and trauma-related nightmares and flashbacks, as well as a decreased sense of safety and detrimental changes in self-image.

_____

_____

_____

_____

_____

To represent these aftereffects, lightly pass over some of the crinkled ridges on the tracing paper with a black chisel-tip marker.

step 4

Let the markings dry. Lay the tracing paper flat on the table. Slowly rub across the surface several times with your hand to soften the crinkled texture. Hold the paper between your thumbs and fingers and continue to soothe the crinkles for another minute. This hands-on action is symbolic of mentally, emotionally, and physically acknowledging, accepting, and soothing the stress.

step 5

Circle 2-3 strengths you've used most in dealing with the severe stress, prolonged crisis, and trauma, as well as the aftereffects.

courage	imagination	open-mindedness	hope	honesty	friendliness	practicality	determination
wisdom	resilience	self-acceptance	faith	integrity	enthusiasm	efficiency	willpower
intuition	endurance	self-regulation	grace	fairness	playfulness	competency	forgiveness
curiosity	adaptability	receiving support	humor	kindness	intelligence	productivity	gratitude
learning	willingness	giving support	energy	devotion	optimism	teamwork	mindfulness
creativity	flexibility	problem-solving	love	patience	spirituality	leadership	humility
bravery	defiance	self-reliance	grit	survival	acceptance	toughness	distraction

Select one oil pastel color to represent the combined positive effects of these strengths. Put a dab of that color in the space above so you'll know what color represents your combined strengths. Set this oil pastel aside for later use.

step 6

Checkmark or circle any of the following wellbeing strategies you have developed and continue to implement since experiencing the trauma. (See Appendix A, page 260, for a detailed description of these practices.)

PHYSICAL SELF-CARE: Attend to your nutrition and hydration, exercise, sleep routine, and physical and dental checkups. Follow through with recommendations from health providers.

SELF CHECK-IN: Identify your emotions. Determine your state of mind. Do a quick body scan. Are you relatively ok in the present moment? If not, what do you need to attend to?

PAUSE / GO SLOWER: Take one or more breaths. Be aware of inhaling and exhaling. Relax tense muscles. Choose patience.

PRESENT MOMENT AWARENESS: Be in the present moment, whether it's pleasant, neutral, or unpleasant. Be aware of what you see, hear, smell, taste, and touch. Acknowledge your thoughts and feelings. Allow them to pass through your mind and body without pushing them away or clinging to them. Be aware of your awareness.

COMPASSION: Acknowledge a problem or difficulty. Give a caring, kind thought and/or gesture to yourself. Know other people in the world are experiencing something similar; you're not alone. In your mind, send compassionate thoughts to those people, far and near.

MULTI-PERSPECTIVES: Look at any given situation from more than one point of view. See the bigger picture.

GRATITUDE: Take time to appreciate what is good in your life. Take care of your life. Take care of what you value in your life.

POSITIVE EXPERIENCES: Be aware of positive experiences while they're happening. Create more enjoyable moments in your everyday life.

MEDITATIVE FOCUS / CONTEMPLATION: If possible, engage in meditation, yoga, tai chi, qigong, prayer, spiritual study, or another inspirational or contemplative practice each day.

DAILY RECAP: Review a difficult moment. Determine what made it difficult. What can you learn from this? What small choice did you make today to reduce your stress or create a positive experience. What are you most grateful for today?

Pick one oil pastel color to represent your wellbeing practices. Put a dab of that color above. Set this oil pastel aside for later use.

step 7

Since experiencing the severe stress, prolonged crisis, or trauma, have you developed greater self-acceptance or self-worth? If so, in what way(s)?

_____

_____

_____

Pick one oil pastel color to represent any improved self-acceptance or self-worth. Put a dab of that color in the blank space below. Set this oil pastel aside for later use in step 11.

step 8

Since experiencing the severe stress, prolonged crisis, or trauma, have you noticed any improvements in your interpersonal relationships with family or friends? If so, what are these improvements?

_____

_____

_____

Since experiencing the severe stress, prolonged crisis, or trauma, have you created new social or supportive connections with people or groups? If so, with whom?

_____

_____

_____

Since experiencing the severe stress, crisis, or trauma, have you intentionally ended any unpleasant or stressful connections with individuals or groups? If so, with whom and for what reason?

_____

_____

_____

Pick one oil pastel color to represent any positive changes you've made in your interpersonal relationship growth. Put a sample of that color in the space below. Set this oil pastel aside for later use.

Have you engaged in any life-enhancing activities that you might not have engaged in if you had not experienced the severe stress, prolonged crisis, or trauma? If so, list them below.

_____

_____

_____

Pick one oil pastel color to represent any positive changes you've made in life-enhancing activities. Put a sample of that color in the space below. Set this oil pastel aside for later use.

step 9

Since experiencing the severe stress, prolonged crisis, or trauma, have you found a greater appreciation for being alive or for simpler ways of being that you didn't have before the severe stress, crisis, or trauma? If so, describe these changes.

_____
_____
_____
_____

Pick one oil pastel color to represent any greater appreciation for being alive or increased simplicity. Put a sample of that color above. Set this oil pastel aside for later use.

step 10

Read through the following list of values.

family	service	success	wisdom	balance	teamwork
friendship	peace	equality	joy	integrity	knowledge
marriage	freedom	prestige	play	bravery	education
commitment	responsibility	career	humor	mental health	recreation
parenting	security	diversity	beauty	physical health	religion
pets	loyalty	generosity	honesty	physical fitness	spirituality
community	justice	love	trust	relaxation	authenticity
nature	creativity	faith	gratitude	meditation	adventure
safety	home	comfort	job	ethical behavior	financial security

Since experiencing the severe stress, crisis, or trauma, have any of your values shifted to bring more satisfaction, purpose, or meaning to your life? If so, describe these value changes.

_____
_____
_____
_____

Pick one oil pastel color to represent any positive value shifts. Put a sample of that color here. Set this oil pastel aside for use in step 11.

step 11

Using the side or end of each oil pastel color you selected and set aside in the previous steps, apply color to the surface of the crinkled tracing paper in whatever way makes sense to you. Review the meaning of each color before applying it to your artwork.

Colors may overlap each other, creating new colors. You may or may not want to smooth some of the colors with a small piece of clean paper towel.

Apply glue in the center of a sheet of white mixed media paper. Place your artwork face down in the center of the white background paper. Smooth the surface, starting from the center of your artwork toward the corners. Apply glue to the underside corners of the tracing paper to secure them.

step 12

In this step you'll be completing a fill-in-the-blanks poem that relates to your artwork.
Following are two examples of writing from artmakers who have previously completed this project.

HOLDING

I held a crumpled wad of tragic expectations in my hands.
Hands that have gathered creativity, faith, and wisdom.
Wisdom to practice self-compassion, awareness, and moments of gratitude.
Gratitude to respect and validate my survival and resilience.
Resilience that helps me to connect with longtime friends and family.
And now, I hold my artwork in my hands, the evidence of my creativity.
Creativity that lets me show kindness, help others, and express what I carry.

EVOLUTION

I held a crumpled wad of brain damage in my hands.
Hands that have gathered endurance and willpower,
willpower to practice self-care and self-acceptance,
self-acceptance to respect and validate my ability to learn and function,
function that helps me connect with other people.
And now, I hold my artwork in my hands, proof of my imagination,
imagination that allows me to be my true self,
my true self that lets me take care of this moment.

On the following page, use the provided prompts beneath the blanks to write your poem. After filling in the blanks, feel free to revise the order, words, and phrases. You may want to delete or add more words. If you wish, write, print, or type your poem on a separate sheet of paper.

_____
(title)

I held a crumpled wad of _____ *in my hands.*
(Fill in this blank with some of the words you wrote in step 1.)

Hands that have gathered _____,
(Fill in this blank with 1-2 strengths you circled in step 5.)

_____ *to practice* _____,
(Repeat last word you wrote on previous line.)   (Fill in blank with 1-2 wellbeing practices you checked or circled in step 6.)

_____ *to respect and validate my* _____,
(Repeat last word you wrote on previous line.)   (Fill in blank with some words you wrote in step 7.)

_____ *that helps me connect with* _____.
(Repeat last word you wrote on previous line.)   (Fill in blank with some words you wrote in step 8.)

And now, I hold my artwork in my hands, proof of my _____.
(Fill in blank with another strength you circled in step 5.)

_____ *that allows me to* _____,
(Repeat last word you wrote on previous line.)   (Fill in blank with some words you wrote in step 9.)

_____ *that lets me value* _____.
(Repeat last word you wrote on previous line.)   (Fill in blank with some words you wrote in step 10.)

Read your poem out loud so you can both see and hear it. Title your poem and artwork if you wish.

LIFE APPLICATIONS

- Severe stress, prolonged crisis, and trauma can be life-altering experiences. It's helpful to acknowledge, accept, and process traumatic events and situations to decrease the possibility that negative aftereffects will dominate your everyday life. Realizing the personal growth that can come from dire experiences also helps to dilute negative consequences.

- In the future, what is one new way you can specifically use your trauma-related growth to benefit your life or the lives of others?

- Review the six categories of growth listed on page 251. Is there one category you would like to focus on now to boost your post-traumatic growth? If so, how will you begin?

- As time passes, you may realize your post-traumatic growth continues to progress. You can repeat this project to acknowledge additional positive gains in your life that have stemmed from extreme stress, prolonged crisis, or traumatic experiences.

CONCLUSIONS

- Note any useful insights, revelations, beliefs, or intentions that emerged while you worked on this project or that come to mind now.

- Detect any tension you're holding in your neck, shoulders, or elsewhere in your body. Consciously relax, pat, massage, or gently stretch those areas.
- If it's comfortable to do so, close your eyes and consciously enjoy three breaths.
- Notice where your body is contacting the chair, floor, or table. Look around the room. Experience a sense of being present in your body and surroundings as you finish.
- Sign and date your artwork. Store it for safekeeping.

APPENDIX A: WELLBEING STRATEGIES

Wellbeing is the sense of being relatively safe and living with a measure of ease. Wellbeing strategies are methods we use to take care of our mental, physical, emotional, social, and spiritual selves.

Review the wellbeing strategies listed below and on the following pages. Checkmark those you're already implementing. Is there a strategy you haven't done for a while that you would like to begin again? Perhaps there are other wellbeing strategies you'd like to add to this list.

Establishing a wellbeing strategy as routine behavior requires effort. Like developing any skill, the more you put a wellbeing strategy to use, the more automatic it becomes. New strategies need to be cultivated by giving them extra attention in the beginning until they're strong enough to grow on their own.

If you would like to do so, choose one of the wellbeing strategies described below that you want to try. Due to individual preferences and abilities, you may not find all the following strategies manageable or helpful. However, sometimes the strategy you initially think is the most undesirable or difficult may be the one that will help you the most.

Make a note of how you want to engage in a strategy you want to pursue. Don't take on too much at once. Go slow at first. You can always build on the strategy as you go forward. Make sure you can readily fit a strategy into your schedule. When, where, and how will you carry out this practice?

If possible, practice this strategy for seven days in a row, then evaluate whether it's beneficial to keep going. If so, how can you customize it to better suit your needs? Do you want it to become a daily or weekly routine? Can you hold yourself accountable or do you need to find a buddy or join a group to sustain your new strategy?

PHYSICAL SELF-CARE

- Plan and prepare nourishing food and snacks. Maintain a balanced diet as much as possible.
- Drink several glasses of water and healthy liquids each day.
- Limit or eliminate high-sugar foods and beverages, as well as other unhealthy substances such as alcohol and recreational drugs.
- Exercise and be active. Move your body at least 20 minutes a day. Stretch, twist, reach, bend, walk, run, dance, or work out.
- Aim for about 8 hours of restful sleep per night. Develop a sleep routine.
- Schedule medical and dental checkups. Follow through with health provider recommendations.

SELF CHECK-IN

- For a 30-second check-in, ask yourself: Am I feeling mad, sad, glad, or neutral?
  Is my mind alert, muddled, disturbed, or calm?
  Am I physically in stable condition or not?

  If you're *not* relatively ok, how can you constructively manage the difficulty in the next hour, day, or week?

- A more precise check-in will help you to further understand your current state-of-being and know how to better respond. Without self-judgment, use the following lists to describe your state-of-being. Select a few or several words that are most applicable.

EMOTIONAL STATE

happy	contented	sad	surprised	angry
amused	calm	lonely	fearful	annoyed
upbeat	satisfied	forlorn	nervous	irritated
delighted	serene	gloomy	anxious	frustrated
excited	peaceful	disappointed	dreading	aggravated
cheerful	pleased	melancholic	suspicious	furious
amazed	thankful	remorseful	horrified	hateful
joyful	mellow	grief-stricken	cautious	rageful
proud	unemotional	sorrowful	frightened	rebellious
blissful	indifferent	heartbroken	threatened	jealous
euphoric	numb	ashamed	disgusted	resentful

MENTAL MODE

alert	confused	conflicted	serious	past-oriented
focused	muddled	day-dreaming	humorous	future-oriented
confident	expectant	mischievous	receptive	defensive
thoughtful	curious	intoxicated	bored	problem-solving
cautious	mistrustful	disturbed	overwhelmed	frenzied
inspired	creative	distracted	intrigued	compassionate

PHYSICAL CONDITION

relaxed	energized	tired	ill	impaired
tense	in pain	healthy	injured	on the mend
awake	sleepy	hungry	thirsty	feeble
infected	debilitated	disabled	weak	allergic
normal	abnormal	stable	unstable	good
strong	ok	unknown	improved	worsening

After acknowledging and accepting your current state-of-being, if it's not necessary to act on any serious problems, return to your activity at hand, allowing your feelings and thoughts to pass through your mind and body without pushing them away or clinging to them.

PAUSE / GO SLOWER

- For a 15-second pause: Take a breath. Be aware of inhaling and exhaling.
  Consciously relax tense muscles.
  Choose to be flexible, tolerant, and patient.

- For a slightly longer pause, engage in one of the following breathing practices.

BREATHING PRACTICE TO RELAX: Inhale fully through your nose. Exhale slowly and fully through your mouth with pursed lips. Repeat 1-3 times.

BREATHING PRACTICE TO ENERGIZE: Stand straight with hands touching your shoulders, fingers slightly curled inward. As you rapidly inhale through your nose, raise your arms straight up. As you rapidly exhale, lower your arms with fingertips to your shoulders. Repeat 6-8 times. Close your eyes. Relax for a moment.

PRESENT MOMENT AWARENESS

- Be aware of what you're doing and experiencing in the present moment. Be aware of your awareness.
- Be open to what is happening now, whether it's pleasant, neutral, or unpleasant.
- Take a moment to notice sounds, smells, textures, tastes, colors, and the quality of light in your immediate environment.
- Instead of being overly concerned about the past or future, focus most of your energy in the present to actively live your life.

COMPASSION

- Acknowledge a problem or difficulty.
- Give yourself a kind thought and soothing gesture.
- Know other people in the world are experiencing something similar; you're not alone.
- In your mind, send compassionate thoughts to those people, far and near.

EXAMPLES OF SELF-COMPASSIONATE THOUGHTS:

This stress is hard for me right now.
It's ok to give attention to myself.
I can get through this safely.
My strengths and values can help me.
I give gentle warmth and caring to myself.
I show up for myself no matter what.
I respect myself.
I'm a supportive friend to myself.
I offer myself reassurance.
I offer encouragement to myself.

This may not be as bad as I think it is.
I let go of unnecessary suffering.
This is how it is for now.
I remind myself that everything is impermanent.
There may be positive aspects to this stress.
It's understandable why this affects me.
I can give myself a break.
I give myself permission to relax.
I offer concern and comfort to myself.
I allow myself to feel hope.

EXAMPLES OF SELF-COMPASSIONATE GESTURES:

Massage my face and jaw.
Pat my head.
Soothe my forehead.
Take a short walk outside or inside.
Drink a glass of water or cup of tea.
Take a soothing bath or shower.
Exercise.
Make a bowl of soup.
Enjoy a healthy snack.
Feel the outside air or breeze on my face.
Take a rest or a nap.
Give myself flowers.

Hold my hand over my heart.
Gently massage my stomach.
Hug myself.
Hold my own hand.
Take a conscious breath.
Read an inspirational passage.
Tap my shoulders with my fingertips.
Listen to comforting music.
Look up at the sky.
Watch the sunrise or sunset.
Go to a quiet place.
Cross my arms over my chest.

MULTI-PERSPECTIVES

- Look at any given situation from more than one point of view. How else can you interpret the situation? See the bigger picture.
- Are you jumping to conclusions or assuming the worst?
- Are past patterns of thinking affecting your current responses?
- Do you need to free yourself from patterns of thinking and acting that are holding you hostage?
- How would someone you respect understand and respond to the situation you're experiencing?
- Things don't always go well but remember that everything is impermanent.

GRATITUDE

- For 10 seconds, appreciate and celebrate the fact that you're alive.
- Start or end each day by reflecting on what you're grateful for in your life. Think about both tangible and intangible things.
- Take care of your life. Take care of what you value in your life.

POSITIVE EXPERIENCES

- For instant positivity, identify 1-3 things in your immediate environment that make you feel contented or joyful.
- Take time to see the extraordinary in everyday experiences.
- Be aware that you're having a positive experience while it's happening.
- Plan and savor enjoyable moments, especially those that are amazing, enchanting, and mind-expanding.
- Seek out new adventures.
- What is one small thing you can do today that will give you a sense of accomplishment or a little bit of control?
- In some small way, take care of one source of joy, beauty, or wonderment in the world.
- Every once in a while, give yourself a treat as a reward or just because you want to.
- Be curious. Be creative.

SELF-ACCEPTANCE / SELF-VALIDATION

- For quick self-endorsement, identify one thing you like about yourself.
- Accept your vulnerabilities, imperfections, strengths, skills, and talents without comparing yourself to others.
- Replace self-criticism with positive and helpful self-feedback to increase self-worth, self-trust, and self-confidence.
- Be your authentic self if it doesn't harm you, other beings, or the environment.
- Remember there is only one YOU in this world.

STRENGTHS

- Use the following list to identify your strengths.

courage	imagination	open-mindedness	hope	honesty	friendliness	practicality
wisdom	resilience	self-acceptance	faith	integrity	enthusiasm	efficiency
intuition	endurance	self-regulation	grace	fairness	playfulness	competency
curiosity	adaptability	receiving support	humor	kindness	intelligence	productivity
learning	willingness	giving support	energy	devotion	optimism	teamwork
creativity	flexibility	problem-solving	love	patience	spirituality	leadership
willpower	gratitude	determination	trust	humility	forgiveness	mindfulness

- Consciously be aware of using at least one of your strengths each day.
- Develop your strengths by using them in different circumstances.
- Combine and use your strengths in new ways.
- Identify a less-used strength and one way you'll apply it today.

SOCIAL CONNECTIONS / SUPPORTS

- Keep up with your network of friends and family.
- If possible, connect with another human being in some way each day.
- Listen, speak, and act with respect and validation toward others and yourself.
- If called for, be assertive but not aggressive.
- Contact supportive individuals and groups when wanted or needed.
- Be supportive. Be kind. Don't expect recognition for your kindness. Be generous.
- Forgive and reconcile when it's beneficial for you to do so.

VALUES

- Select values below that are most meaningful to you. Consciously live by them every day.

family	service	success	wisdom	security	teamwork
friendship	peace	balance	joy	integrity	knowledge
marriage	freedom	prestige	play	bravery	education
commitment	responsibility	career	humor	mental health	intelligence
parenting	financial security	diversity	beauty	physical health	religion
pets	loyalty	generosity	honesty	physical fitness	spirituality
community	justice	love	trust	relaxation	authenticity
nature	creativity	faith	gratitude	meditation	adventure
safety	home	comfort	job	ethical behavior	equality

- Make decisions and set goals according to your values.
- Focus on your own priorities, values, and goals, not on what someone else thinks is important.
- When you live your values, you may also be helping humanity and the world.

MEDITATIVE FOCUS / CONTEMPLATION

- For a one-minute reflective break, read a short inspirational passage you have readily available.

- If it's helpful to you, engage in meditation, yoga, tai chi, qigong, prayer, spiritual or philosophical study, or another form of inspirational or contemplative practice each day.

- It's important to note that not all types of meditation are helpful for all individuals. Some people who have experienced trauma may find that stressful memories, emotions, and flashbacks arise when practicing sitting meditation without a concrete method to stay grounded. A more structured approach to meditation, such as tai chi, qigong, yoga, walking, or art and writing formats may be a better fit, as these methods involve bodily movements or activities to sustain physical and mental focus in the present. Find a meditative practice that works for you.

- With any form of meditation, thoughts and emotions will naturally arise while you're meditating. The goal of meditation isn't to stop thoughts, it's to become aware of them and then gently return your focus to the practice.

DAILY RECAP

- Review a difficult moment. Determine what made it difficult. What can you learn from this?
- Remember that making mistakes is part of actively living our lives and being human.
- What small choice did you make today to reduce your stress or create a positive experience?
- How did you use one of your personal strengths today?
- What are you most grateful for today?

APPENDIX B: NOTES FOR THERAPISTS, COUNSELORS, AND GROUP FACILITATORS

Individual Therapy

- When appropriate, you can recommend this workbook to clients as a supplement to therapy sessions.
- Alternatively, you can select a particular project for a client based on issues coming up in therapy. Any project can be done as homework and brought back to the following session to discuss. You can also have clients work on the project in session to observe and offer support during their process.
- When discussing clients' artwork, it's recommended you refrain from interpreting the art in any way, even if clients ask you to do so. Although you may have certain thoughts on meanings attached to lines, colors, shapes and imagery, your meanings might be quite different or even opposite to those of your clients. If clients feel you are analyzing their work, it can stifle open exploration, impact trust, and prevent them from doing the work they need to do. Help clients explore and discover what the artwork means to them by asking questions and encouraging discussion about the overall artwork, details within the artwork, their writing, and the creative process. Encourage and allow clients to make the connection between their artwork and their lives.
- The projects in this book were carefully designed to offer an experience that is creative, reflective, grounded, and constructive. If at any time clients become overwhelmed or unstable when engaged in artmaking, writing, or discussion, take a break. A deeper, paced discussion about what is coming to the surface might be important if this occurs. Each project can be done in stages, returned to later, or a different project can be chosen.
- If possible, complete a project yourself before asking clients to do so. This will increase your understanding of what clients could experience and instigate a more thorough discussion about the clients' creative processes and products. It's highly recommended that you refrain from doing these projects in session at the same time clients are doing them. It's important to be fully attentive to your clients during therapy sessions and not distracted by engaging in your own personal work. As you probably already know, it's not helpful to discuss your personal artmaking experiences or products with clients.

Groups and Workshops

- Group participants can complete a project in a group session, or they can complete a project at home and bring it to the group to share.
- Two-hour group sessions are ideal if participants are completing and sharing art projects in the group. If time runs short, creative writing segments can be finished at home.
- As the group facilitator, you're in charge of pacing the group, keeping it on track, handling overly disturbing subject matter that may negatively trigger other participants, and ending on time. Set a tone with participants to encourage comfort and safety. Participants count on you to oversee and guide the group process.
- Complete a project yourself before asking the group to do so. This not only helps to prepare and plan timing for group sessions, but also increases your understanding of what group members may experience.

- Art materials required for all projects in this workbook can be easily transported and a sink or water source is not necessary. It's helpful to have cleansing hand wipes available to clean up when using oil pastels and glue sticks.
- For projects that call for found images, it can be beneficial to remove and precut images from used magazines (art and photography magazines are particularly rich image sources), books, newspapers, brochures, catalogs, old calendars, greeting cards, etc., before the group meeting. This will save group time and prevent distractions since the images are readily accessible and the participants don't have to search through numerous sources for images during the artmaking portion of the group. Images may be abstract, semi-abstract, and realistic, depicting colors, shapes, lines, people, animals, indoor or outdoor scenes, natural or man-made objects, art reproductions, and other visual elements. Do not offer violent or sexual images. You may want to make multiple photocopies of images or online printouts to have on hand if you frequently facilitate groups.
- If a project calls for found papers, provide an assortment of used bags, maps, envelopes, notebooks and pads, wrapping papers, art papers, handmade papers, various waste papers, or any paper product that will adhere with a glue stick. Papers may be printed with words, patterns, or other designs.
- Display precut images, assorted found papers, and solid-color paper on a separate table or counter away from areas where artmaking is occurring to allow easier access for participants and less mess.
- At individual artmaking stations, place tools and materials necessary to complete the project: scissors, glue sticks, writing pencils, paper towels, ultra-fine pen and chisel-tip marker, white mixed media paper, and tracing paper. Participants can share boxes of oil pastels if necessary.
- The group process can generally follow the project's structure. You may want to start the group by presenting some of the points in the project's introduction, adding any information you feel would be helpful.
- Let participants know there's no right or wrong way to do art, art skills aren't necessary, and the quality of their artwork isn't important. You may need to demonstrate art techniques in the group for clarity. Keep an eye on participants during the artmaking time in case anyone is having trouble and needs support.
- Before sharing artwork, mention that feedback should be positive and constructive, never critical. Participants should refrain from interpreting each other's art or writing. Quality comparisons among artworks aren't helpful to anyone. Tell participants they're each a valuable part of the group no matter how much they wish to share. Some people need to reflect longer before sharing; some need to maintain tighter personal boundaries. The group experience can still be very therapeutic even if a participant chooses not to share. Having this stance often results in greater participation and a sense of safety within a group.
- Pace the art-sharing part of the group carefully so those who wish to share have equal time to be heard. Before sharing, let participants know approximately how long each person will have, so they can respect time limits and won't be offended if time limits are enforced by the facilitator.
- At the end of a group session, encourage participants to take their artwork with them. Looking back at their artwork and creative writing can help them glean additional insight. You may want to provide paper folders so their artwork is protected.

ACKNOWLEDGEMENTS

I'd like to thank Jim Rankin whose patience and skills lasted through several rounds of proof readings and edits. Appreciation goes to Cherrie Lucerne-Martin, who volunteered many hours in the early stages of developing some of the projects for this workbook. I'm also grateful to all the clinicians who have authored books and articles and have spoken on theoretical principles and practices that were both inspirational and instrumental in the making of this workbook. And finally, a sincere thanks to teachers, colleagues, clients, artists, poets, and numerous others who have contributed to my life experiences and subsequent knowledge relevant to the material included in this workbook.

Anita B. Rankin

Many thanks to my mother, Shannon Rupp Barnes, who gifted me with an upbringing rooted in kindness, integrity, service, and unconditional love. My husband, Don Fibich, my sons, Jack and Will, my siblings and their families, provide unending support in all areas of my life. I have also been fortunate to have brilliant teachers and colleagues over the years who shaped and inspired my work as an artist and art therapist. Lastly, for 35 years, I have worked with individuals, young and old, seeking out personal growth and healing. It has been an honor to witness all the ways creativity brings them closer to where they want to be.

Mary Michola Fibich

ABOUT THE AUTHORS

Anita B. Rankin, MA, ATR, CPT, is a registered art therapist and certified poetry therapist who specializes in trauma treatment with individuals and groups. In addition to co-authoring the book, *Managing Traumatic Stress through Art*, she has published articles on art therapy research and treatment approaches in professional journals. Anita has taught graduate classes in art therapy and trauma treatment at The George Washington University, presented at conferences, and worked with therapists to manage their work-related stress. She has volunteered at the DC Rape Crisis Center and with the National Organization for Victim Assistance following mass-casualty and natural disaster emergencies. She is active as an interdisciplinary artist, has taught design, artmaking, and poetry writing; and has juried, curated, and organized art exhibits. Anita currently lives with her husband and rescue dog in Tucson, Arizona where she continues her decades-long meditation practice and more recent endeavors with tai chi.

Mary Michola Fibich, MA, ATR, is a registered art therapist, professional artist and poet. She has worked in the art therapy field for over 35 years in trauma, psychiatric, addiction, hospice, educational, medical, and corporate settings. She is the co-author of the book, *Managing Traumatic Stress through Art*, a valuable resource for the public and therapists for over 25 years and a featured artist and poet in the book "Portrait of the Artist as Poet." Mary has facilitated numerous workshops and professional presentations focused on art therapy, trauma treatment, grief therapy, therapist self-care, and personal wellness at both regional and national conferences. She has worked as a consultant since 1996 in human service and corporate settings utilizing art therapy to manage stress and promote team-building and human development in the workplace. Mary is a fiber artist and painter. Her art is featured in both private and commercial collections throughout the United States. She lives in the beautiful state of Maine with her husband and two sons.